In the Face of Death

In the Face of Death

LOUIS EVELY

Translated from the French by
Camille Serafini, S.C.N.

A Crossroad Book

THE SEABURY PRESS / NEW YORK

1979 * The Seabury Press
815 Second Avenue * New York, N. Y. 10017

Originally published as *Questions de Vie et de Mort* by Les Presses de
L'Imprimerie S.E.G. 33, Rue Beranger, Chatillon-Sous
Bagneux, 1978.

Printed in the United States of America

Library of Congress Cataloging in Publication Data
Evely, Louis, 1910-   In the face of death.
"A Crossroad book."
Translation of Questions de vie et de mort.
1. Death.   I. Title.
BT825.E9513   236'.1   79-16993
ISBN 0-8164-0442-9

Contents

In the Face of Death

CHAPTER 1

Modern Man Confronting Death

In wishing to live without dying, one dies without having lived.

To reflect upon death, is to reflect upon life. Death is a dimension of living, it forms a part of life as the estuary forms a part of the river; it is our most faithful companion, the only one which never abandons us and which may arrive at any moment.

Let us dismiss the illusion, moreover, that it will come to us from the exterior, from an accident, from an unknown cause. From within us, as a fruit, we bring it to maturity. It is the outgrowth of what we make of our lives, and we are prepared for it by countless partial deaths, by countless hours of sleep, by countless exhalations. At each choice, at each parting, at each death of a friend or relative, a little bit of us dies.

From birth, we begin to grow older and to die. True youth is the embryonic stage when we benefit from an amazing dynamism that we will never again experience for we grow much more rapidly during early years than in the latter part of life.

Ultimately, to refuse death is to refuse life. In order to live fully, one must have the courage to integrate his death with his life. This is not a question of obsession, but simply of an extension of the field of consciousness, of not refusing to see

what is displeasing to us. Living seems so natural that we do
not believe it possible for it to discontinue. We all know that
we will die but no one admits that death concerns him per-
sonally. Jouhandeau wrote: "During half a century, I did
not age beyond twenty years. The moment has arrived for
me to give up this usurpation." But he is entirely too modest
in speaking of a half-century. We all live as if there were no
end. Old age takes us by surprise and the thought of death
clashes against an insuperable incredulity.

In playful moments, we toy with the idea that we will have
to die but only to better measure how distant death is from
us, how foreign to us it is, and to reassure ourselves of still
feeling so alive.

Even the death of a contemporary, wholly admissible as it
may seem to us, we lay to a particular cause, a concurrence
of circumstances ("what did he die of?"), an exterior aggres-
sion: he should not have had to die, he should have been
able to live. Only the death of someone we love so much that
he forms a part of us, will occasionally tear away these
querulous responses.

The attitude of man confronting death has always been a
mixture of attraction and denial. Basically, we realize that
life is fragile, that life is haltered by death and that it strikes
at any age. However, we repel this obsession by a will intent
upon disowning death, our death. "If anything ever happens
to me" ventures that elderly person, that invalid, that mortal!

I remember the astonishment of the young recruits in the
Resistance when they saw our first dead. All their enthusiasm collapsed. They had never imagined it possible.
Henceforth, they must fight for more serious reasons than
those which sufficed when they believed themselves immortal.

Likewise, I had, up to then, judged last moment conver-
sions as suspect, unfair, as if through fear one abjured what
he had honestly lived. But the experience of combat has

modified my opinion. What happened at death, was not, above all, the invasion of fear, it was the evidence of a reality always previously denied and rejected.

Negation of death dazzles us with delusions, distracts us from reality, prevents us from living a truly human life. The reintegration of death into life is a necessity for humanization.

As long as I believe myself immortal, I do not have to choose what occupies or entertains me. I have "plenty of time." The thought of death introduces a summons to choose, to question. "What is essential for me?". It requires a transcendence. "Do I have what is needed to confront death? What is life, and what is worth more than life?" To reflect upon death, is to learn how to live.

*   *   *

Apparently there was a time altogether different. The thought of death was familiar to the point of obscuring life. People preached on death, they meditated on it, they delighted in multiplying images of it, and long before death they prepared themselves for it. The decadent religions, estranged from daily realities, specialized in the invisible and the hereafter.

Notwithstanding so much discoursing about death, people perhaps did not believe in it any more then than they do now, but the fear and the promise of another life, nevertheless determined their behavior.

Our contemporaries act as if they were never going to die. Our ancestors conducted themselves as if another life, more important than this one, exempted or prohibited them from living. It is impossible for a youth of today to realize how much man was then haunted by hell and damnation, heaven and its marvelous rewards. Life was used to prepare for a good death. Madame de Sévigné regretted not having died in the arms of her nurse. "That would have relieved me of much anxiety, and would have so easily assured me of heaven" (16 March 1672).

A few years ago, some elderly ladies invited me to speak to them, and the organizer prompted me: "I hope that you are going to prepare them to die?"

I was shocked. "What, prepare them to die? But the poor creatures are already too dead! I am going to encourage them to live, I am going to prepare them for life without end. I want to awaken them from their torpor, invite them to think of others, alert them to the beauty of the world, to a love of all which they have loved and are still capable of loving.

"I will say to them: 'Your husbands who are waiting for you, do not want an old woman, a dead woman. They want you living, young of heart, loving, and to be sure, happy, open to others, to nature, to music, to poetry, interested in events, in the evolutions of your times.'

"I will ask them: 'Do you have enough with which to live? If to die, is to expose oneself to what one experienced on earth, do you have the wherewithal to furnish your eternity? Do you have enough with which to live forever? The morticians in the United States ask on billboards: 'Have you enough to die?' because their help costs so much. But one may understand the question otherwise: 'Whom do you love enough to live with forever? What moments of your life do you wish to perpetuate? If you die tomorrow, what will you take with you, what will you immortalize with you? Be, right now, the way you would like to be always! Establish immediately, with those around you, the relations which will delight you eternally!' "

Up to that point, these old ladies had been piously occupied in severing the ties which attached them to life. They had shrunk into a circle which was more and more reduced in occupations and interests and they thought that their renunciation of all that they had possessed was a sign of their disposition for heaven and the price to pay for entering therein.

There is only one preparation for death. It is to be so alive that one can live forever. Do what you will, but do something that is good enough to last forever!

What keeps us alive is the number and depth of our interests, of our relations. We live only from our communications with others, with the world. Death is insupportable if it separates us from everything. Are there any creatures to whom you are more attached than to yourself? Do you have bonds which resist all separation, a love stronger than death, a faith which has revealed to you how good and just it is to entrust yourself to it beyond all security?

Today

Our age is the first in history to live without the two fundamental values which have dominated all the preceding: God and future life. Today the masses are disinterested in God to a degree where atheism actually seems more normal than faith, and they deny afterlife to the point of juggling away death.

But, of these two estrangements, the one opposing the hereafter has grown more rapidly than that regarding God. For anyone who reflects, it will seem astonishing that 80 percent of the French population still wants churches in the center of new cities, particularly since only 73 percent admit the existence of God, 35 percent believe in a hereafter and 21 percent in the resurrection of the dead.

In England in 1963, a poll revealed that 17 percent of the women and 3 percent of the men interrogated on their way out of the cemetery still considered that final farewell as an "until I see you again in the next world." (Fabre-Luce: *La mort a changé*).

Our contemporaries no longer believe in what rendered death bearable, which explains why the natural tendency to resist the idea of death has become aggravated to the point where we systematically reject the very reality of death from our minds.

People remove the dying. In America and in England, 80 percent of deaths occur in hospitals. And even in medical environments everyone is forbidden to speak of death, they hide the dead, they act as if death did not exist.

Professionally, the doctors, nurses, technicians work to prolong life, to force death back, and notwithstanding their remarkable success, they always end up conquered. This contradiction is painful for them to endure and it is natural that they mask their unavoidable failure. Moreover, the death of a human being confronts each of us with his own death, and who among us is disposed to welcome this warning serenely?

Dr. Elisabeth Kübler-Ross tells how she searched to establish a dialogue with the dying in order to do a psychological study. In a 600-bed hospital, she was told that there was not a single dying person. As she insisted, the authorities objected that the patients were too sick, or too weak, or that they did not wish to talk. Finally, they ushered her out of the hospital.

But when, at her first encounter with an aged person who had shown his desire to speak with someone of his death, she proposed to sit down and start immediately, only to be put off. "Oh no, not now, tomorrow, at one o'clock!"

The doctors hesitate to enter the room of the dying, the nurses seek a pretext to leave as soon as possible. Each one acts out the farce. The medical personnel plays the game of attention and treatment, always inventing something to do in order to avoid confessing powerlessness. The relatives play the game of hope, and the dying person is obligated to play the game of health.

A young woman who was dying at a hospital where she was studying wrote:

> I am a student nurse. I am dying. I write this to you who are, and will become, nurses in the hope that by my sharing my feelings with you, you may someday be better able to help those who share my experience.
>
> I'm out of the hospital now—perhaps for a month, for six months, perhaps for a year—but no one likes to talk about such things. In fact, no one likes to talk about much at all. Nursing must be advancing, but I wish it would hurry. We're taught not to be overly cheery now, to omit the "Everything's fine" routine, and we have done pretty well. But now one is left in a lonely silent void. With the protective "fine, fine" gone, the staff is left with only their own vulnerability and fear. The dying patient is not yet seen as a person and thus cannot be communicated with as such. He is a symbol of what every human fears and what we each know, at least academically, that we too must someday face. What did they say in psychiatric nursing about meeting pathology with pathology to the detriment of both patient and nurse? And there was a lot about knowing one's own feelings before you could help another with his. How true.
>
> But for me, fear is today and dying is now. You slip in and out of my room, give me medications and check my blood pressure. Is it because I am a student nurse, myself, or just a human being, that I sense your fright? And your fears enhance mine. Why are you afraid? I am the one who is dying!
>
> I know you feel insecure, don't know what to say, don't know what to do. But please believe me, if you care, you can't go wrong. Just admit that you care. That is really for what we search. We may ask for why's and wherefore's, but we don't really expect answers. Don't run away—wait—all I want to know is that there will be someone to hold my hand when I need it. I am afraid. Death may get to be a routine to you, but it is new to me. You may not see me as unique, but I've never died before. To me, once is pretty unique!
>
> You whisper about my youth, but when one is dying, is he really so young anymore? I have lots I wish we could talk

about. It really would not take much more of your time
because you are in here quite a bit anyway.

If only we could be honest, both admit of our fears, touch
one another. If you really care, would you lose so much of
your valuable professionalism if you even cried with me? Just
person to person? Then, it might not be so hard to die — in a
hospital — with friends close by.

Dr. Elisabeth Kübler-Ross, Death: The Final Stage of Growth, pp. 25-26

A reaction is setting in at the present time and people are
beginning to recognize the necessity of psychological aid to
the dying, more realistic than making them believe that they
are not going to die.

What must be done to help the dying? Must one tell the
"truth" to the patient? Surely not! It would be inhuman to impose *our* truth on him. And moreover, who is sufficiently sure
of his diagnosis to dare condemn a patient? Some, who were
to have died in six months, have lived ten or fifteen years.

But it is necessary to tell them the truth. Do not delude
yourself. They know, or suspect it; they have a presentiment
and they wonder. Many good people have told me regarding
their dead: "He did not realize anything. He was not conscious of his condition. He did not know that he was dying."
But, was it not they rather, who needed not to speak of it?
Very often the sick person, at heart, knows. But he has no
one to whom he can speak. No one lets him talk about it and
he himself does not know how to approach it.

Let us not wall the dying into silence by avoiding their
timid, often symbolic advances. Let us not increase their
fears by the contagion of ours. Let us not leave them alone,
let us not anticipate, by our avoidance, the death which is
soon going to separate them from the ones they love.

Certainly, let us encourage them until the end; leave them
some hope (because it is true, there is always hope); let us
nurse them without uselessly prolonging their sufferings, but

let them confide in us their anguish. Let us accompany them
to the end, and in a certain way, let us die with them.

It is by confronting our own death, by entering into this
depth of communion with them that we will be helpful.
What causes the most fear, is not always death, but being
left alone to live out the hour of dying.

The same obsession explains a certain therapeutic des-
peration. They sustain in apparent life irrecoverable coma-
tose states in the name of the sacred character of life. As if
physiological life were human life. As if there were interest
in prolonging unconscious agonies. As if a man unable to ar-
range his life at a given moment, does not prefer to be allowed to die in peace. As if human life were sacred to the extent
that one never has the right to renounce it or to make use of
it. And those who proclaim life untouchable at its beginning
(abortion) or at its end (euthanasia) are often the very ones
who sacrifice it at its highest development (war, death
penalty).

It is understood that in our time, which is universally ad-
mitted to be without supernatural values, people are tempted
to make sacred, to absolutize existence and to recognize this
limit to the fanaticism of ideologies, to the radicalism of class
tensions, to the harshness of power struggles. But human life
is not the supreme good and one does not become truly
human until he has discovered that for which he is prepared
to sacrifice his own life — and also even why it is lawful to resist
to the point of sacrificing that of others.

*　　*　　*

Evidently it is not only in the medical spheres that the
signs and presence of death are expelled. People no longer
wear mourning; cemeteries are being located farther and
farther away (formerly, graves crowded around churches,

and, even closer, the privileged were buried under the floor). Dead bodies are concealed or, in America, shown all made up like the living.

How long has it been since you saw a corpse? Many children have never seen a dead person, never seen anyone dying, perhaps not even a sick person. The taboo on death has replaced the taboo on sex. People are presently engaged in introducing children, from their early years, to the "mysteries of life," to pregnancy, birth, contraception, if not to abortion. Yet they systematically hide the dead and the dying from children, and maintain silence when questioned about death, as formerly they did when children asked how babies come into the world.

Besides, we would be much embarrassed in answering them. The old forms are arrested on our lips, and we do not know any better ones: "God took him... God came after him... He is beside Jesus in heaven... It has pleased the Lord to call him..."

Then we change the lie: "Grandmother is on a trip" or "She is resting in a beautiful garden." As someone has said: "Babies are no longer born in cabbages, but the old disappear among the flowers!"

We parents who think ourselves liberal impose on our children an education as despotic as that practiced by Buddha's father. He jealously guarded his son from knowledge of sickness, suffering, old age and death. It was the belated discovery of them that determined the ascetic and extraterrestrial vocation of Buddha. He was brutally initiated for he learned one day, by chance, what no one among his fellow citizens, what no one among us any longer knows because of routine or of repression: that he was going to die, and he never wanted to forget it.

What spiritual awakenings, but also what psychological traumas this modern education and our consumer society promise us. But especially, what widespread anguish our fears and falsehoods prepare for our children.

* * *

A ridiculous and unavoidable fashion obliges us all to pretend that life always tends towards more life, youth and joy. We wish to look young, beautiful, invulnerable, and because of this we set aside the old (we conceal them in hospitals, we rid ourselves of them in nursing homes). We remove the sick, enclose the handicapped, drive them from the streets (by our cruel reactions of curiosity or of disgust: "such people ought not be be seen!") We bar them from business, from human relations. The dying frighten us, the sight of a corpse is unbearable to us, we locate the poor beyond the beautiful neighborhoods. But we accept the rich, even though they be old, ugly, obnoxious, because their money reassures us. The image which they reflect of ourselves does not dishearten us, alas! They have the real modern antidote: money. Even adults are devaluated in our day because of our obsession with youth.

What an alarming contraction of humanity. And what folly. I do not wish to speak ill of young people, they constitute our hope, however, often they disappoint us. We turn toward them in order to perceive the countenance of the future, and, thirty years from now, they will experience all our trifling concerns of the past. Certainly they are apt in discerning errors and in denouncing falsehoods but they are rarely capable of discovering the truth for themselves and of creating something new.

Their irresolution is praised as if it were a valuable security.

Their want of sincerity, of activity, of justice, of friendship is an excellent motive for them to react against an af-

fluent and technical civilization. But they are too inex-
perienced, too weak, and too inconstant to achieve their
aspirations without the aid of adults. They stimulate us by
their criticisms, and we are indispensable to them in propos-
ing accomplishments in which they can believe and in en-
couraging them to invent in their turn.

We adore youth and money because in them we look for
security. The expression "poor old man" sums up all the
contempt of the world, the total wretchedness. Poverty was a
beatitude in the gospel; it has become the definition of
misfortune. He who no longer has youth or wealth is without
protection against what we most fear: death.

But what a mocking protection: there are youthful deaths
— and there is no lack of death among the rich.

*   *   *

But "poor" and "old" deflect us from the image we seek.
They hold up a mirror in which we refuse to recognize
ourselves, a likeness which we decline to acknowledge as our
own. In these expressions, we refuse to see ourselves as we
are, completely handicapped, poor, weak, frail, mortal.

As a result of rejecting the image which innumerable people present to us, we no longer possess a human
countenance. We wear only the mask imposed upon us by
our pretenses and our fears.

By force of wanting to conform to an artificial model, we
are becoming strangers to ourselves. By force of avoiding all
creatures who remind us that we must die, we create a desert
around ourselves. By force of driving weakness and death
away, we reject life.

Human life is fragile, vulnerable, mortal. There is no
human life without a certain acceptance of death, without a
certain familiarity with it. We commit suicide rather than
see ourselves mortal.

On the whole, is not the fear of dying and the boredom of living the characteristic of our age? From boredom we escape by noise, speed, sex, drugs, revolution, and even by work which permits thinking of everything except ourselves. ("If I were not so lazy, I would not work so much. If I were not so distressed, I would stop now and then. If I were not so afraid to live, I would take the time to live.")

The mediocrity of individual existence creates the disposition for great collective adventures. On the eve of May 1968, Viansson-Ponté wrote: "France is bored." The most terrible thing that I have seen at the approach of wars, was the relief of men who, despite some dreadful happening, looked forward to liberation from their perpetual ennui. The war was to sweep these individuals without familial, professional or religious attachment, effortlessly towards the trenches, the concentration camps, the cemeteries.

The youth of the present time live in suspense. They are ready for the best and the worst. Nothing will stop them, neither terrorism, nor torture inflicted or endured, nor dictatorship, nor catastrophes, if only they be cured of their boredom, if only they may again find the taste for living.

For want of something better, the secret motive for many apparently generous commitments is the need to alleviate the burden of personal existence by an affiliation with movements which relieves them from the trouble of searching for themselves. Commitment is a snare when it exempts us from our responsibilities, when it merges us into a community which thinks for us, when we no longer bring to the cause which we serve, the contribution of our criticism, our initiative, our personalities. Surrender of initiative is no more than an aspiration towards death, and this desire becomes compulsion in those who have fled death too resolutely.

The great need, the great modern business centers on

diversion. Actually there is only one complete, perfect and uninterrupted diversion, and that is death. Hitler offered this magnificent adventure to German youth. What a stupendous movie he had them live, this course of an entire people from despair to triumph and from triumph to despair. In the darkened theater all those strained, livid faces turned towards the screen which shines like a pebble under water. And over there in the vast plains of Russia, all the upturned, rigid faces, immobilized in their final abstraction. Basically, did they really want anything else but this perpetual vacation outside of themselves?

"He who wishes to live without dying, will die without having lived." To accept a day of death is to find again the truth of the human condition. What refreshment would we experience if we disarmed ourselves of our artificial protections, if we entered into the companionship of the poor, the old, the sick. They are our image, our recovered truth. In recognizing them as humans, as sisters and brothers, we would receive from them in return the disclosure of our own humanity, so beautiful in its misery, so touching, so vibrating with life in its frailness. "Despise not your own flesh!" says the prophet.

If you have taken care of the sick, sat up with the dying, associated with the handicapped, visited the old, you know what wealth of humanity resides in them. These beings that we put aside in our desperate desire to be immortal are the ones who are able to restore to us the relish of friendship, of tenderness, of compassion, of simple joys given and received.

*   *   *

Recently, a handicapped infant was born into a friend's family. What do you think was the first reaction? Rejection!

It is terrible to find yourself bluntly confronted with such radical weakness. The parents were hoping to find each other again in this prolongation of themselves, to contemplate themselves with pride and complaisance in the mirror of their infant. Instinctively love is very egoistic. Mainly, we love only ourselves, only that which resembles us. Woe to the abnormal (because, we are the normal ones). Woe to the deformed (because we are the models). Woe to all those who are not liked by us, as we imagine ourselves to be.

We want our children to show our vitality, our richness of life, our generative strength. We want to be able to recognize ourselves in a flattering image of ourselves.

So, before this large-headed freak, this strange creature, weak, restless, we refuse despairingly to see ourselves as we are: handicapped, weak, frail, mortal. A passionate desire is to disown it, to remove it, to put it out of sight, perhaps, to kill it with the complicity of the attendants, who are as horrified as we, before this disillusion. The parents did not dare to show their child to anyone, they did not dare to speak of it to anyone, they dared not think of the future, they dared not envision what their life would be with this caricature of all their hopes.

Little by little, they have accepted. They have had to react with all their strength against what is instinctive and possessive in paternal and maternal love. They have had to pass beyond their aversion, their fears, their shame. They have had to struggle against society which hates the handicapped, that terrible society which, at Liège, after the death of little Carine Van de Put, a victim of thalidomide, applauded the parents who had killed their infant.

Gradually, they have learned to recognize themselves in their child and in accepting it as it is they have learned to accept themselves as they are, and to acknowledge in the infant a humanity which at first they had denied. In the beginning, they regarded it as a monstrosity, a stranger who inflicted itself disagreeably on their family intimacy. But like themselves, their child cries, suffers, calls out for protection, for acceptance, for love. And one day, they saw it smile in recognition of them, they, who had not recognized it. They have learned from it all the cost of each development, of each stage of life. And they have agreed that it is not like them, nor like others, but that it is itself.

Take care, those of you who rejoice in discovering yourselves in your children. Your illusion will be of short duration. Soon they will rebel, they will cry out that they do not wish to prolong you, that they are not just extensions of you, that you are searching vainly in them for a means of believing yourself immortal. They will show you in every way that they do not resemble you and that they will have their own life. They will let their hair grow, they will dress in tatters, they will refuse to wash, all in order to assert that they are other people, that they are not you, that they will leave you some day just as you are, old, feeble, mortal—that condition, which you do all you can to refuse.

The only difference between the parents of the handicapped and us, is that they had to understand immediately and we take ten, fifteen years to learn that our children are not ours, that our children are not identical to us, that they belong only to themselves and that nothing, not even they, will exempt us from dying, from having to accept death.

If we became human again, we would no longer fear dying. Because to accept death, is already to admit the possibility of a meaning to death. So long as we deny it, so long as we yield to fear, we affirm that death has no meaning, that it is inviable, hateful, inhuman. But to admit it, is to consider death as a question for which it is possible to find an answer.

He who does not assume his death lives a suicide existence, an unbearable existence, because he refuses an essential condition of life.

But only one life is needed to attain that condition.

Let us measure the scandal of true Christian Revelation. It proposes a wounded God to us, a handicapped God, a God who dies. A God who is incompatible with our mad hope of immortality, who teaches us to die, to live mortally, to live as men.

Until then, God had fled the human condition, projecting our longings into an invulnerable, sovereign and inhuman image both of himself and of us. But Jesus restores us to reality. It is by living our human existence like him until the end, death included, that we will draw nearer to the mystery of God.

A human God invites us fraternally to die with him, with everybody, to link our fate to his and to theirs. He reveals to us that the essential does not lie in our aspirations towards him, in our communications with Him, but in our human relations — those which we maintain with the poor, with strangers, with the sick, with prisoners, with all those who need us, those whom we need in order to be ourselves.

It is not God who will save you from eternal death, it is the friends you make and who help you discover that you are able to abandon beauty, youth, money, everything that was indispensable to you when you did not love.

Only love enables one to face death. Because love is already a kind of death through which one learns to consider as nothing that which was formerly esteemed and to open oneself to the Other, to enter into the world of another, to pass into another world. If you have loved enough, your death will resemble your love.

Opening oneself to death is like opening oneself to love. Both require a going out of self, a finding of self in going beyond ourselves, in surmounting our fearful limits, in entrusting to the hereafter our securities and possessions.

A hereafter beginning today.

*   *   *

Modern youth makes fun of its parents who wondered: "Is there a life after death?" "Is there a life after birth?"

But, is this not the modern form of the rich young man of the gospel's question: "What must I do to acquire eternal life?" Not a future life, you will notice, but a present life, one to be lived immediately.

And Christ did not answer: "Prepare a good death for yourself." But "leave everything and follow me." In other words: "Risk your life on a personal relationship; learn to love and to live. All riches are dead weight. They sterilize you, fossilize you, immobilize you. I am going to lead you into a life stream, on to a life adventure, into an intensity of life which will never end." That which makes us live is not our ties with things, but our relations with persons.

We do not live from having; we live from being. Others have over us the same influence that we have over them: the power to make us live and that of making us die. "Speak to me, or I die," said a certain woman to her husband. "He still assures me of my living, but he no longer makes me live," said another. Death is a separation, the loss of our relationships. He who loves no one, no longer needs to fear death. He is dead. He is living in a mortal indifference.

We are all so tempted to consider our security as dependent on our possessions that for a long time I considered, in the response of Christ, only the first part: the renunciation, the sacrifice, the detachment. "Sell all that you have" measuring the effort asked of me.

I needed experience in order to place stress on the invitation: "Follow me." What an unlimited future it opened, what discoveries, what genuine enrichments! "Accompany me, entrust yourself to me, learn another kind of life than the one which you have lived so poorly until now. I am going to show you other ways, other occupations, other horizons, other friends: all those whom Society, your Church, your

money have excluded: the poor, sinners, foreigners, prisoners who should be liberated, the sick who should be cured,
the dead who must be resuscitated, and (from that time on,
but more certainly in our day), women. Once you have
yielded to the love which is offered you, nothing will be of
comparable value and you will not even know how to regret
what you have lost."

In reality, is it not an invitation to death as well as to life?

And notice still another thing. The young man had
observed the commandments since childhood. He had been
well raised, educated in a good college, nourished in a good
family. . . and he was totally sterile. All of that had failed to
give him life.

Religions have gone astray, and we have strayed by reason
of entirely withdrawing ourselves into the interior and into
the hereafter, in our strivings for an individual and spiritual
salvation, "save one's soul." In the face of modern atheisms
which are doctrines of earthly and community salvations,
the influence of Churches has collapsed.

But to what extent this ruin is due to their infidelity, one
will judge by this same gospel. The rich young man emerged
from a model religion, the exact one which formed the
average believer in spiritual aspirations, moral prohibitions
(neither contraception, nor divorce, nor abortion, nor
euthanasia, nor homosexuality, nor masturbation, nor
preconjugal relations), with a *secret, but fierce attachment
to riches.*

Now the Kingdom inaugurated by Jesus was totally different. It was in the world, in life, "in the midst of us." It in-
tegrated all outcasts, those without hope, the borderline
people, those excommunicated by Churches. The only
message which the Apostles were obliged to deliver to the
cities to which they had been sent, was the Good News.
There are no longer any chosen people it declares, no

privileged ones, no favorites. The Kingdom of God is for
you, with you, in you. Discover, establish among you this
Kingdom by satisfying the poor, by incorporating the rejected, and by overturning the social classes. Let the poor
possess the land, and let the rich, the powerful be at their
service.

The Beatitudes proclaim: Blessed are you who are
hungry, you will be satisfied. Blessed are the meek, you will
possess the land. Blessed are the poor, for the Kingdom of
God is yours.

That is to say: Blessed are the poor. You are going to
cease being poor.

And we have interpreted: Blessed are the poor, remain or
become poor.

Let us admit that, as Good News, there is better.

The new life, the intense life, the animated life which
Jesus promised to those who followed him, was this overturning, this revolution: the establishment on earth of human
relations which are so just, loving and profound that they
are able to perpetuate themselves and enable one to meet
death.

Until this meeting, the young man had believed in observ-
ing the commandments, that sin expelled God and that it
was the absence of sin which rendered God present and
which procured true life. But Jesus taught him, on the contrary, that it is the presence of God and of his brothers and
sisters that would drive away sin and introduce him to Life.

CHAPTER 2

A Meaning to Death

In this matter [survival], not to examine in depth what others have said, and to give up knowing before one has done all that one is able to do, is the characteristic of the apathetic and cowardly. For it is absolutely necessary, to learn well from another what it is all about, or else to discover thoroughly for oneself, or, finally, if these two methods are impossible, to choose among all human reasonings the one which seems the best, the most difficult to disprove, and then to risk oneself on it as on a skiff in order to make life's passage...

Plato, Phaedrus

Urgency for a Meaning

"Man," says Voltaire, "is the only animal who knows himself to be mortal," and one is merely man, if in face of this mystery, he has discovered, if not how to resolve it, at least how to bear it.

Man formerly found this support in a social and religious environment which determined for him his position, his duties, the direction of his life. It constituted a kind of maternal bosom, a social uterus from which he could grow, mature and die without anguish.

Today, man has pulled down all his props and risen from all his obeisances. He is standing upright, but he is alone. God is dead and self-mastery is disappearing. The technocrats abuse the environment as the artists deform and dismember objects. Man has become God and so there remains nothing before us that we can admire or conquer. We have been reduced to ourselves and forced to exert our own destructive techniques over ourselves. By not recognizing what is beyond us, we are falling into insignificance.

Man is a sharing being; he needs to unite himself to a complete reality. Solitude destroys him utterly; it is a premature death. He doubts everything if he can believe in himself only. He agonizes if everything depends solely on him, because he himself is searching for something to trust, to believe in. He knows that he will die before having understood and transformed this world for which he is claimed to be responsible.

The drama of our civilization (is there actually, a civilization? Are we not rather, speechless, between two civilizations, one which is collapsing, and the other which is searching for itself?) is that it offers no universally-accepted values in which to believe, to which to devote oneself and with which to identify beyond death.

Why are the churches not more successful in effecting the acceptance of the explanation of death, which for ages they propagated with singular success? Turned back upon themselves and the past, they are hardened like so many institutions whom inspiration deserts and who put their confidence in the solidity of their edifices. A too long habit of believing has imperceptibly congealed into a habit of not believing. Life has contracted into dogmatic formulas similar to the ecclesiastical institutions. After having given life to preceding generations, the churches have been dethroned by newer and more dynamic movements (scientism, fascism, communism) which have centered interest on the present life and on the changing society, leaving to the churches the interior and future life.

Alas, after these great hopes, rapidly subdued, after a blaze of joy followed by cruel awakenings (two world wars, Auschwitz and Hiroshima), life continues in a stupor. The ideologies have worn themselves out as completely as the religions but much more quickly. We have passed from elating Utopias to complete disaster. The end of the world is being predicted by ecologists, antiatomists, anticapitalists, anticommunists, sociologists (population explosion) and geophysicists (aridity), whereas the structuralists prove that the man whom we think ourselves to be has never existed.

The young people, disgusted with this consumer society (from which however, they benefit without remorse), incapable of supporting an existence without horizon, are restless and searching in all directions for a doctrine, a master, a Transcendence to give meaning to their lives.

Finding Ourselves

We will have recourse neither to God, nor to Revelation in order to establish a reasonable confidence in another life. The Christian doctrine assures us of the resurrection of the flesh and of eternal life, but it is not a question of our reciting formulas, not even of accepting them on the word of others. In so grave a matter, one must not rely on anyone's assertions. One must listen in order to interiorize and verify the statements. The contents of an idea are never just the experience which they convey, the progress which has been accomplished at their encounter. Christ himself told us that he who puts his word to the test of practice, will prove if it comes from the Father. The internalization and the personalization of faith have caused, by default, the present crisis of Christianity. Let us hope that they will be the fruit of it.

A true faith is not founded on the testimony of others. It

requires that the faith itself be a witness of what is attributed to it. The gospel says: "Come and see." This faith also demands witnesses who are sufficiently clear to make new witnesses of that to which they testify. For it is no longer because of what you say, that we believe. We have heard it ourselves, and we know that he is truly the Savior of the world.

God does not testify, God does not speak. The men who speak are always those who have had impressions of God. The only basis of faith is this impression of God, this movement of the Spirit which reaches out directly across the intermediaries and makes me say: "Should God not be there?"

These impressions of God are difficult to interpret and to control. One must feel one's way, guided by common sense, by others and by experience. All "revelation" is affected by a measure of incertitude proportionate to the lucidity and receptivity of the witness.

And in addition, has God ever revealed anything to us that we should not have been able to discover on our own by knowing ourselves better? If God reveals himself, does it do anything else than to make us feel his dynamic presence in our utmost depths? Do you think that God intervenes at special moments, through privileged interpreters, by enunciating dogmatic propositions, or better still, that he manifests himself at each moment, to each person, commensurable to that person's receptivity? Do you think that God limits his gifts and the distribution of them according to his good pleasure, or that the only limit to his generosity is our resistance?

In this highly important domain of death, it is childish to entrust yourself to assertions, to promises or even to past events. You may consult everybody, but ultimately, you must listen to yourself, provided it be in depth. You are the only one who believes what you do, I mean to say, you are the only one to translate your convictions into the formulas of others.

What is, for you, the last test of the truth? A man, a book, a community? No, it is the truth, which no one either possesses or can deliver to you ready-made. And in the same way, only you can discover and recognize it. Finally, the sole criterion of what is true, after the exhaustion of all verifications, is you.

"But," you will say, "I believe in God's Revelation, in Jesus, in the Church, I believe in my religion."

"Yes, but it is not enough to believe because you decide that it is right to. Therefore, before believing in whatever it may be, believe in yourself. And, moreover, you only believe in whatever you have understood of what God, Jesus or the Church says. Progress in your faith will come only from development in your assimilation.

And if, in this teaching, something seemed evidently false or immoral to you, you would suspect that it has not been revealed, because *you*, cannot acknowledge it.

Besides, the idea of availing oneself of a Revelation on these universal problems shocks me. I do not wish to pride myself on a supernatural or unverifiable knowledge. I want to search, with all of mankind, for human truth. What God speaks to us, I believe that he says to everybody because, if he exists, he is the truth for all, the truth of life.

I often have recourse to the gospel, not as to a sovereign authority, but as a human experience of inexhaustible richness. A Revelation can only enlighten us as to ourselves — and every deepening of selfconsciousness is a revelation.

Faith does not adapt itself to evidence, nor to ignorance. With evidence, you know, hence you do not have faith. With ignorance, you do not have the right to express your opinion. Faith is having enough insight to support you through obscurities, enough answers to carry you through questions, enough experience to confront the unknown, enough gratitude to give you confidence in what may come.

But one often forgets that the unbeliever on the fundamental problems of the existence of God, of death, of survival, is in exactly the same state. How deny with certitude that of which one has no conclusive experience? How be certain of the nonexistence of a being or of a fact which escapes our knowledge? How is one to show that God or the soul cannot exist?

We have no experience of real death, and of what happens after death. *One can only speak of life.* It is from it that one must set out to search for that with which to confront death. Do we, or do we not have, the experience of a life, which biological life can neither give nor take away, of a life which does not fear death, over which death has no grasp, of a life on account of which one would be able to die at once, and with which one could live forever?

All of life is a construction, a realization of self, to the degree where a certain dissociation takes place between this life which is truly ourselves, and the biological life which permits this realization of self but also limits it and finally deserts it. The desire for eternity is simply the perception of our spiritual nature disengaged from all which conceals it and that is why every human, in his heart, knows himself immortal.

By the same token, has belief in an afterlife been spontaneous and universal since paleolithic ages? Natural certitudes ought to be questioned. They are a mixture of errors and truths. The entire aim of reflection is to transform these certitudes from common sense into good sense (which has nothing common about it).

But is it not already good sense which, before a corpse, confirms a terrible "absence"? Death cries out to us that there is something within us that is not to be confused with our organism, that there is a "residue" manifestly different from the remains. We establish undeniably, an awful difference between a corpse and the presence of a person but nothing gives us instruction on the persistence of this notion. The dead person's absence might be only a disappearance, but what is there to assure us that it is not a question of an annihilation? Only one opening remains, a possibility that must not be neglected.

No Future Life

We are no longer speaking of a "future" life. Only the present life concerns us, and in this, the problem of the quality of life. Future life is the opium of the people. It is a hoax which makes one await in the future, a change which would neither be produced or at the least prepared in the present. True Christian faith is a faith, not in future life, but in eternal life. A moment of reflection suffices to let us comprehend that it has begun. We are living it now or else we will never live it.

It is only when life acquires a singular quality that the question of death becomes of prime importance. For the primitive mentality, man is so totally inserted into his family, his village, his people, that his death only makes a fusion into the ensemble. The permanence of all that counts more than any single person renders his disappearance insignificant. In certain tribes, the individual is only distinguished by his occupation. At his death, if someone inherits his work, his successor takes the name and the "spirit" of the dead. The clan has regenerated its lost member. The individual neither knows nor desires any other survival.

But the person who knows himself to be unique cannot accept this self-annihilation, not by reason of egoism or fear, but through respect for his personal value.

False Deaths And The Real One

We also reject the easy solutions proposed by certainties, i.e., death is similar to sleep from which one awakens refreshed each morning, or it is a painful delivery, but one which gives birth to a superior life. "There is no awakening without sleep," we say, "no inhaling without exhaling, no return without a departure. Every choice is a self-denial. Living, without dying a thousand times, is it living?"

It is easy to answer that there are two kinds of death, and that it is important not to confuse them. One is beneficial and necessary: it is a passing, a development, a going beyond. But the other is sterile as much as it is loathsome to us: it is an uprooting, an abortion, a destruction.

In the vegetal and animal world, there is no real death, only transformation without annihilation.

What is extraordinary in our condition, is not the dying. It is that nothing seems to spring out of this disappearance, nothing appears to be reborn from this cutting away. Death of a human being is absolute, a dead loss, useless sacrifice, shocking waste. This unique creature, of inexhaustible singularity, this being has lived so little what he actually is, that no one has known him because he was entirely different from what he let us see of himself. He was a being, whom no one loved as much as he wanted, because his need of and capacity for love grew in proportion as people loved him more.

Man dies a double death: biological death can occur prematurely, accidentally, but is not a destruction, and personal death which causes stupor, rebellion, and scandal because it ushers in an absence without remedy.

It is a great temptation to confound these partial deaths with that complete death and to promise to the dying a metamorphosis for which examples are all borrowed from experience of partial deaths.

There are "illusions of death" which one must face and go on, but there is an actual death, an evil one which seems to end our existence without opening out into another. Before death it was a matter of choosing, and indeed all sacrifice in life is, in a certain manner, a sacrifice of life. But this sacrifice was counterbalanced by a quick move of life into another realm than the one in which one had accepted the necessity to die.

We are counseled to make an act rather than a resignation of our destiny, to take it upon ourselves rather than to submit to it, but is this not just trickery, if ultimately nothing results from the difference in conduct?

In order to undertake your death, you must know what is to be gained by dying, towards what you are going, who is welcoming you. If a despot offered us the choice between casting ourselves into a fire or of being thrown into it, could it be said that we were assuming our death while economizing on executioners? It is not a question of assuming or not assuming death, but of having *the wherewithal* to go beyond it.

Signs of a Transcendence

We suffer from an essential unevenness between our being and our life. We are so rarely the person we would like to be. We habitually move about like amputees of ourselves, as much strangers to ourselves as to others. We never accomplish that to which we aspire. We do not love as we would like to love. We have never said what we wanted to say. Vainly, we try to reunite ourselves, to coincide with our yearnings. As Simone de Beauvoir says: "One searches to be and finally only succeeds in existing."

How can we experience such a dissatisfaction, if there is not within us a veiled presentiment of a perfection to which we compare the miserable results which we attain? Rimbaud declares: "True life is elsewhere." But to know that it is not here, one must perceive it as repressed but active, working.

We are in life, and at the same time we are spectators. We have the strange faculty of measuring our lived life by the standards of another life, which should be a living life. In the consciousness of every person there appears from time to time an uncanny Mene—Tekel—Peres. Nebuchadnezzar decoded it, with the aid of Daniel, whom he had judged, weighed and found too light to survive. Each human discovers at appointed moments that his life does not measure up. It is lifted from him then and there by the single vision of a person, of a cause, of an idea in which he rediscovers himself infinitely more like himself than that to which he has dedicated himself, than in everything which he had valued up to then.

Each human arrives at freedom when he feels that he could decide to die. Each person, sooner or later, encounters that for which he would like to give his life.

We live two lives, one judges the other and ascertains the discouraging distance which separates them.

"I have loved a life which I have not fully understood, a life, not entirely faithful. I do not even know very well what I lacked: it was a light hunger..." says one of Saint-Exupéry's heroes, and he continues, "What I was becoming hid behind everything. It seemed that with effort, I was going to understand, I was finally going to recognize it and carry it away. And I went away, troubled by that presence of a friend that I was never able to draw out into the daylight..."

Stop a sixteen-year-old youth and say to him: "The hour has come, you are going to be judged. Here is the good you have done, there is the evil you have committed. The tribunal is going to decide." His reaction is foreseeable. "But I have not yet begun to live. I have been submissive, I have had patience, I have waited. Now that my horizon is opening out and I am going to be able to realize my dreams, you lay claim to stopping me. It is too unjust! Nothing of what I have done is like me."

Stop one at thirty years, will he not say the same thing? And at sixty? "Life has not yet allowed me to be myself. I have not expressed myself. I am continually waiting for the setting, the circumstances, the encounter which is to set free in me that wave of love and talent which weighs upon me. My life has been too short, but from one moment to another, I am always hoping that it is going to begin."

In the Bible, we are told of a patriarch, several times a centenarian, who left this testimony: "The days of my life have been short and wicked." And Rilke complains, in his inimitable tone: "No one lives his life. People are unpredictable. . .it is their mask which speaks, their faces are silent. . .each one tries to break away from self as from a coffin which loathes and encloses him."

We detest our existence and we hold on to it with equal tenacity. We detest our insensibility and we preserve it as a defense. We detest our fears, and we withdraw in order to avoid suffering. Love, faith, and hope are inherent to the soul, and the soul never ceases to combat them.

We are at the same time in the world and out of the world, in life and out of life. We are not of this world and our life is not the true life. There is within us a *relentless dynamism* which makes us exceed all that we experience. We are compelled to search for a direction in this world, a meaning to life in this world which will permit us to surpass it, to go out beyond it.

Our spirit is too boundless and we will never have finished exploring its resources. One has noticed countless times, in front of a work of art that we identify ourselves in it, that we are set free from something that we carried within us unconsciously, that we discover the infinite extent of our needs. All is within us, not as a fixed object, but as an energy which seeks to exert itself. It is a nobility in mankind to need all the poets, all the musicians, all the artists in order to hear himself singing, praising.

The best compliment that one can address to a writer, a musician, an artist: "You have expressed what I have always vaguely felt. You have brought me into an area of myself from which I was excluded. I did not know myself before having met you. You have cleared, populated, liberated in me an entire dimension which remained mute and empty, and which is however, the one where I best discover myself. Of your genius, I know myself incapable, and yet nothing is more natural to me."

The great work of God in Christ, is in short, nothing but a Revelation. Jesus did not bring us "supernatural" talents from the exterior. He did better. He revealed us to ourselves. He spoke to us as no one had been able to speak, but as we needed to hear. He reached us at a depth where no one before him had had access, of which we ourselves were unaware, but which he rendered vital and free by declaring it.

Solzhenitsyn makes the dying Chouloubine say:

> And sometimes I know so clearly that what there is in me is not yet the whole me. There is something else which is very, very indestructible, something very, very lofty! Something akin to a burst of the Universal Spirit! You do not experience that?
>
> Alexander Solzhenitsyn: *Pavillon des Cancéreux (Cancer Ward)*, p. 710

We are a part of *nature,* and yet we rise out of it. We keep a distance from it, caused, at the same time, by awkwardness and superiority, by a goodness and cruelty which are not encountered in the animal world. The other creatures are at ease in nature. Man does not succeed in blending into it, and that is why he creates, while the animal repeats. He invents an environment suited to his uniqueness and he discovers himself at the same time. He claims kinship with another world yet complains of being exiled. At certain moments nature becomes insupportable, so indifferent is it to our pains and to our desires. Man is essentially a creature of queries, of posing questions, a being for whom not all is incontestable. Is it not natural that he would question even his own death? In the animal and vegetable world where creatures replace themselves without truly disappearing, death vindicates itself. But man is not a simple object of nature, his specificity is evident. This perception which emerges outside of nature, and liberates us from it, how could nature be capable of lifting us from out of itself?

Man is made to live in *society*. He opens and expands not only thanks to it but also by asserting himself against it. He labors to preserve and better it, but finally, it is society which is at his service, and not he who serves it. For only the individual is conscious of himself. That is what makes him superior since consciousness alone defines us as human beings and of that other species are deprived.

Death is at the service of the lesser species. It assures them of variety and of renewal. But man, freed from the species by his thinking, wants also to free himself from death, necessary to the species, but fatal to human beings.

We are both in *time* and beyond *time*. If we were entirely within time, we would glide along with it without noticing. Now, we assist in its flight. We are simultaneously on the street (passing by) and in the balcony (seeing ourselves pass). We would not know that the time is passing if we were moving along entirely with it, no more than we would notice a change of place if everything else were moving around us at the same speed. Movement is observed only in comparison to a stationary point.

One does not become conscious of the passing of time unless something in us escapes into it. "From what would we be conscious of death," asks Olivier Clément, "if it were not from eternity?"

When you hear a sentence, you do not really understand it until it is completed. That presumes that in your interior span, you would preserve as simultaneously present all the words of the sentence which have been uttered successively in the exterior duration. Which means that there is something in you which is beyond time and which alone permits you to understand what is within time.

If you were completely in the exterior duration, you would coincide with each word and you would not even know that there had been a succession of words (since, for that, you must still hear the past words while listening to the present word).

"But," you will say, "I preserve them in my memory."

Yes, but if your memory were material, it would have to preserve and recall them as they had been pronounced, that is to say, successively. Now in order to understand the sentence, it is necessary to have all the words present simultaneously.

There is then within us a nontemporal present where we gather elements successively furnished in time. In this manner we assist an unfolding without wholly participating. We are in time, seeing that we experience the action, and beyond time, since we synchronize the results.

To understand a symphony, a play, a novel, is to gather together again what happened over several hours. We comprehend outside of time what has occurred in time. Since the past and the present are equally present to us, it is because we are, in a certain fashion, independent of time. (Valensin et Zundel)

Likewise, when I wish to translate a text from one language to another, from French to English, for example, I must mentally retain what the French is saying, but lay aside some of the French words. I compare, I try the English expressions of the idea in some way stripped of its diction, as if I were capable of a pure idea independent of words, of matter, of time.

One might imagine eternity as a presence (before oneself) of all the experiences of one's life, of all that one had desired and loved during the course of one's existence. "Do you have the wherewithal to furnish your eternity? Do you have enough with which to live (eternally)?" are questions sometimes trivially asked. One should add: "Do you have the wherewithal to die?"

We feel ourselves alone, and it is because we only live from *relations* and exchanges. A person is formed and developed by the network of his bonds. "It is in the interior of another's perception that the consciousness of self unfolds ... The source of the me is the you." (Maurice Nédoncelle: *La Réciprocité des consciences*)

Without relations, the child remains an animal, a wolf-child who lives only an organic life. But it awakens to its own humanity at contact with its mother, its father, its neighbors, school, its country, the world, and if it has a religion which will establish a global conception, of its ties with the universe.

We become ourselves only thanks to others. They have given us birth but at each moment still, they are necessary to place us and replace us in the world, to free us from this interior weight which oppresses us (and is perhaps, an overflow of love and talent), to bring to light the best within us, to liberate us from all that we have not yet succeeded in giving up.

It is only when others recognize us that we begin to exist.

From necessity we cry out towards others, and need for them
terrifies us. Others have over us the power of life and death.
They make us live, if they love and welcome us, they kill us if
they forsake us. That is why so many among us prefer to die
immediately in order to be dependent no longer, to wait no
longer, to suffer no longer.

How hard it is to maintain oneself only by dependence on
the unforeseeable generosity of others, to await indulgence
from their "good graces." Our security depends on others;
our happiness depends on others and we are at their mercy.
"Speak to me, or I perish," is the mute prayer of each one of
us to each other, a prayer which one dares not formulate for
fear of exposing oneself to a refusal.

Nothing equals the fear and the desire which this vaguely
felt truth stirs up in each one of us. It is as difficult for us to
provide for ourselves as it is painful to free ourselves. And
yet we all know that the most precious moments in life are
those when we have experienced the most intimate communion with others, and we have all felt that separation,
isolation, is the worst of punishments, the foretaste of
damnation.

The real death, the unacceptable death is the absence of
communication, that separation from others, from
ourselves, from that interior source of inspiration and love
which we call God.

Nevertheless, the awakening of consciousness of self,
establishes between us and nature, people and life, an insuperable distance which creates a terrible anguish. This
can only be remedied by love and communication, which
are not lasting conditions but rather a struggle and a victory
over incomprehension, coldness, and petrification.

"The awareness of our solitude," says Mounier, "is the
perception of what in us has not yet been spiritualized." Our
real mode of communication (the body, the senses) is as

much a screen as a means. It holds us apart as much as it unites us. How can we not desire a more intimate, more direct, more satisfying union? Belief in God is, basically, believing in a source of infinite communion. "God," says Rilke, "is a control given to love."

*   *   *

This duality between man and nature, man and time, man and species, man and others, man and himself, clarifies the meaning of man's death. Biological death is a necessity for the species. But our death can be a fulfillment of the person. We are at length going to expose ourselves to what we have lived, so little and so poorly. "To die," writes Gabriel Marcel, "is to open ourselves to what we have lived on earth." Let us understand that it is not a matter of rediscovering what we have lived, which depends more on circumstances than on choice, but of realizing this aspiration for love, for admiration, for creating, for prayer, of which we have been fashioned and which gives direction to our existence.

We can never reflect sufficiently on this fundamental fact: man has always acted as if something else surpassed human life in value. Consciously or not, we are forever comparing the lived life to the true life, our actual willing to our desired will, immediate objects to our deep-seated appetite for infinity.

Assuredly man has been mistaken on values or rather he has identified too quickly this superior value with life beside his leader, with his country, his religion, with a cause, or with money. But what remains, under all these labels, is the undeniable presence of this power in us, and even of this desire to surmount biological life, to sacrifice it. Man has always had such an esteem for, and so strong a presentiment of true life that he has sacrificed himself, often too easily, and he has searched in death to become identified with his spirit which is beyond all his accomplishments.

The law of the animal and vegetal world, is the ferocious struggle for life, with victory going to the strongest. The most characteristic law of the human world is the sacrifice of life, at times in the service of the weakest.

I have seen men die for a cause. They radiated life and joy. They knew with inmost certainty that the body was nothing of them, that their earthly life was unimportant in comparison to that life which animated them and which was immune to bullets and blows. They experienced, certain ones of them for the first time, the prodigious reality of the spiritual life. They lived by it from then on and forever.

Indeed, many among them did not think explicitly about survival. They only felt that whatever might happen, it was a good thing that they had done. In any case, they would begin over again. They had reached a state where no regret was possible.

With a humility much more real and more striking than what is experienced by those who resign themselves to a complete disappearance, they did not even think of an afterlife. But if they had been questioned, they would have affirmed absolutely the value of what they were doing.

They did not claim a reward, they subordinated themselves so passionately to the cause which they served that they were no longer distinct from it. They were so much a part of it that they would not have been able to assert it or deny it. The nature of the spiritual life by which they were living appeared so clearly to them in these moments that they could no longer call themselves perishable.

It was not through fear, nor through interest; it was solely through love that they recognized themselves as invulnerable. They had discovered something so good as to wish themselves alive, to know themselves to be alive because of it.

There is no immortality for the person who is not passionately alive. There is no survival for the person who has found nothing to love. Love alone knows that he will love forever.

It is this experience of participation that Saint-Exupéry admirably describes in *Pilote de Guerre:*

> People have taken so much care of the body! They have dressed it so well, washed, groomed, shaved, watered, nourished it. People have identified with this domestic animal. They take it to the tailor, to the doctor, to the surgeon. People suffer with it. They cry with it. They have loved with it. People say of it: it is I. And behold, all at once this illusion collapses. They laugh heartily at the body!
> ... Your son is caught in the fire? You will save him! He cannot be held back! You are burning! You do not care. You are leaving this garment of flesh in pawn for whoever wants it. You find that you no longer value that which was once so important... You? It is the rescue of your son. You give yourself in exchange. You do not experience a feeling of loss in the exchange... The fire has not only caused the flesh to fall but at the same time, the cult of the flesh. The man is no longer interested in himself. Only what he really is asserts itself. He does not withdraw, though he die: he merges. He is not losing himself: he is finding himself. This is hardly the wish of the moralist. It is an ordinary truth, an everyday truth, that a common illusion is covered by an impenetrable mask... It is only at the moment of giving up the body, that all, always, discover with stupefaction how little they value the body.

Is it necessary to specify that this spiritual life is not a simple prolonging of ordinary existence, a simple survival which will be for the most part, more of a threat than a promise. It is an above-life, a super-life, the continuation of only that life in us which transcends time, space, egoism.

Let us not confound it with the instinctive and pitiable need of safeguarding one's existence and of retaining one's possessions, an attitude wherein there is no more nobility than in the nonchalance to nature's law, in the animal-like resignation to our common fate.

To actually confront death is to accept an unlimited stripping, to yield to an awful transformation, to fling oneself headlong into a new existence, to renounce one's possessions and habits in order to place one's trust in the unknown.

Faith is never without doubts, nor death without anguish. Our most important decisions, choosing a profession, getting married, giving birth to a child have always been options which immensely exceeded the reasons which we had for the decisions.

Conclusion

Our life is without common measure with what we feel within ourselves as better. We can neither renounce it nor succeed in accomplishing it.

The fundamental experience of man is the tragic insufficiency of life and of that strange faculty of withdrawing ourselves from it, because we can experience another kind of existence which we compare with it and which detaches us from it.

Art, love, duty, prayer are the windows opened onto infinity.

Art is the denial of nature, the creation of an excessive universe, the expression of our nostalgia, a beginning of withdrawals. Thanks to art, we attain an invulnerable state, independent of life's accidents, a world which corresponds to our dreams and which we must, nevertheless, constantly leave.

There must be, between Beauty and ourselves, a communication so deep-seated that we are much affected when we meet it, that we uproot all that is not beauty, that we search for it everywhere, that we suffer from being deprived of it, that we recognize it clearly when it presents itself to us.

Morality is not purely rational. It has a mystical foundation, for it evokes an unlimited agreement. Its real assent is in the interior of the soul. It is not a question "of putting oneself in order." One must find oneself in giving, one must have discovered an Absolute which allows one to surpass everything. The Czechoslovakian philosopher, Jan Patocka, signer and martyr of Charter 77, wrote:

> No society would know how to function without moral assistance, without a conviction which does not result from opportunity, circumstances and expected benefits. Morality does not exist in order to make society function, but entirely, to allow man to be man. Man does not determine it according to the arbitrariness of his needs, his wishes, tendencies and desires. On the contrary, it is morality which defines man . . . The notion of an international pact for the rights of man signifies nothing other than this: countries and society place themselves entirely under the sovereignty of moral sentiment. They recognize that something unconditional governs them, surpasses them.

Love establishes between two people much more than a life community, a participation in the same creative liberty, in the same discovery of a hereafter. Love is the passion for going out of self in order to find oneself.

All true love is an opening onto death through impatience with our limitations, an ecstasy where one can live forever and for which one is able to die immediately. Love feels itself eternal.

To pray is to arrive at a new level. It is entering into a strange zone but always with premonitions, offering oneself

to meet Another. One must calm oneself, rouse oneself, remain silent in order to allow the deepest sources to spring,
filter, and burst forth.

Prayer is a death and a resurrection. One dies to the
troubled and noisy part of self, to one's thoughts, to one's
unawareness, to one's ambitions, and one is born to another
life, another view, another Will. One is born to a depth
where before one knew only death.

But they who have succeeded in remaining insensible to
these appeals are those who have not loved, not prayed, not
admired, not listened to any other voice than their own. To
them, there remains the final urgency to transcend themselves. Inevitable death questions them, presses them, summons them: "In what and in whom do you place your confidence? Where are your treasure and your heart? Are you
hung up on your past or are you open to your future? Do you
clench your hands on your possessions or do you extend
them open as do the poor? Do you try to defend yourself or
do you agree to trust?"

No one escapes this last interrogation and perhaps no one
resists it. There are people who have contended unceasingly
against a proposition of faith or love, against a humble and
tender presence which has given to their life all its kindness,
all its warmth, all its visible richness, and yet to which they
have never wanted to open themselves. Then at this last moment they understand that they are going to lose it for the
first time and forever and that they have known nothing better than what they have always rejected.

One does not know what transpires in the depth of a person with all distractions and escapes discarded and what is
the real face under all those masks by which one has pro-
tected oneself.

Rilke says this in obscure and magnificent language, but
how can one speak clearly of mystery?

A father (Michael) stays up all night beside the body of his suicide son, of his son who has disappointed all his hopes, who has disgraced himself by base acts:

And behold the day, when the great sorrow which had remained seated near him silently, takes him into its custody, and we see how in the hands of sorrow, he is transformed . . . The old man does not speak, he grows, and it is like the quiet murmur of growth. He discovers himself infinitely strengthened. The treasures which he himself was unable to extract, death has released for him. The ugliness on the face of his son, was but a reflection. Death has snatched off all the masks, opened all the Persian blinds and revealed everything. And Michael knows that he was not mistaken: his son was surely there, he *is* there. His body is not an empty chest which he scarcely wore in life until he presented it as a newborn, before eternity. These are treasures without measure that he carried, with trembling arms, and life did not touch them, life did not open the chest — life spent none of these riches, it did not discover them. For life is blind and without requirements. But death has displayed all . . . death, this most merciful form of life.

CHAPTER 3

Reflections on the Christian Meaning of Death

Let us, from the very first, dispose of some obsolete disputes. In the nineteenth century, people accused Christians of resigning themselves to present evils in the hope of a future life. Yet they congratulated them on having the good fortune to believe and pretended to envy them because their faith was so consoling.

From that point to suspecting them of believing for their own reassurance is but a step. Moreover, the Christians retorted, meanly enough, that if their adversaries rejected the afterlife, it was through fear of being punished!

Let us not reduce such a problem to a question of courage or of fear. More people are reassured by nothingness, nonexistence, than are driven to despair. They do not insist upon eternity, especially, if it is spiritual. The body and its pleasures gone, they would willingly accommodate themselves to sinking into unconsciousness. Did they not long ago form the habit of entertaining themselves, of escaping themselves, of absenting themselves? They live so sparingly that they have become accustomed to oblivion. "We have our whole life for diversion; we have all of death in which to rest," chants Moustaki.

It is not of death that people are afraid, it is the expiring; but once dead, let them rest in peace, that is their whole desire. Whereas, faith disquiets by the uncertainty of the fate which awaits us.

In fact, experience proves that on an average believers and unbelievers die according to their temperaments, rather than according to their convictions. The worriers draw new motives of concern from their beliefs and the confident elicit reasons for serenity.

Likewise, let us recognize that faith in another world has deterred certain people from struggling to better our world. Moreover, haste to enjoy the present life has had the same results. But, the believers respond, and many have given proof of it in deeds, that their faith is lived in the love of their brothers and sisters and necessitates the transforming, rather than the evasion of this world. Will you be more stimulated to better this world if you believe that everything you do will be destroyed someday, or if you are assured of perpetuating what you have loved?

Vain polemics, between atheists who reproach Christians for firmly believing in a surmised hereafter, and the Christians who ask why they are so sure of nonexistence in a beyond which they have explored no more than they.

One might be irritated by the cutting tone of Montherlant on this subject, if one did not guess the anguish under the exasperation.

A life comes to an end like the last smoke rings of a cigar which is burning out. The preceding rings are already undone; the cigar will die out; nothing remains of the rings. Every other conception of life is bla-bla-bla and deception. Henry de Montherlant: *Tous feux éteints*, p. 53.

I understand that survival is doubted, but I am astonished that it is denied with so much assurance. You have sided with total death? That of others? Your own? But is it not a "prejudice" rather than a certainty, a manner of concluding the inquiry and of stifling the uneasiness? Have you decided the nature of the spirit and the boundaries of life, or have you only set a limit to your research? Does not the present-day conformity in favor of destruction resemble that with which formerly people professed faith in the resurrection of the body?

Let us acknowledge that it is always a matter of option. Each person decides, each one must decide for reasons but where reason does not play the only part.

Some agree to die positively, and even in a certain manner, immediately, in order to bury the problem. They close themselves to the unlimited, to the possible, to questions. Others, take refuge in convictions which are too arbitrary to be profound.

Would it not be fair to say that both believers and unbelievers agree to call into question, the ones their faith, the others their incredulity, and both of them admit their doubts.

*   *   *

Catholic teaching on the "last things" (heaven, hell, purgatory, limbo), formerly, so thunderous in the exercises of "Mission," is becoming more and more discreet. Parallelly, the competent listeners are becoming fewer, I am not saying of believing in them, but of being interested, and the preachers themselves are sufficiently convinced of this lack of interest as not to dare speak of them.

Our age has discovered that theology has responded foolhardily to a lot of questions whose depths were not measured and which were stifled rather than resolved.

What happens after death?

Progressively, life helps to form a human being. Does death destroy his life or does life simply disappear from our eyes?

Most certainly, qualities of the mind are different from those of matter so one may imagine that it is not destroyed with matter, but the mind in an isolated state is inconceivable. How could a human being subsist without his brain, without memory, without this means of communication with the world which is his body?

Our contemporaries, philosophers and scientists, consider less and less spirit and body as divisible. Two things can be distinct and yet incapable of division. The form of a discourse differs from the subject matter but how separate them?

Man does not *have* a body and a soul; he *is* organized matter. His body is as essential to him as his soul.

Many are even inclined to think, with Teilhard de Chardin, that in each particle of matter there already resides a certain consciousness, a tendency, given characteristics. In proportion as matter organizes itself, new properties appear, physical qualities at first, then life, then a superior complexity, the spirit.

Finally, one may imagine that in the beginning a chaos of matter was created as well as a spiritual dynamism charged with progressive integration of the matter. Have you noticed that man, with his nervous system resembling fuses, and his accumulations of carbon in the muscles, similar to explosive reserves, is so programmed that the minimal impetus produces important physical effects? One might say that the body is calculated in such a way that the spirit has minimal difficulty in propelling it into action. Prisoner, up to the point of organizing the body's matter, man's spirit finally liberates itself of its servitude, becomes conscious of itself and expresses itself independently.

Our understanding of the beginning and the end of existence would be upset.

For a long time, the traditional thesis which posited a special intervention of God to create life at a certain stage of evolution, then to create the soul at a later period, seems ridiculous to our contemporaries. What is to be said of the

Catholic doctrine according to which God collaborates at each fruitful embrace of spouses for the particular creation of the soul of the embryo. Berdiaff writes:

> The traditional, theological opinion according to which the human soul was created by God at the moment of physical conception is so lamentable that it is not worth the trouble to pause there seriously... It is indispensable to admit the preexistence of the human soul in the spiritual world...
>
> Nicholas Berdiaff: *Esprit et Liberté (Freedom and the Spirit)*, p. 342

This theological stance will become still less admissible when scientists succeed in creating human beings in a test tube in a laboratory. With more and more difficulty, we call on God to explain the happenings of the world.

At the other extremity of existence, when this particular organization of matter, which constitutes man, is worn out, what will subsist of the spirit which the matter had permitted to become conscious of self and to act? If the spirit continues, will it be infirm as it was before expressing itself through the body, somewhat like radio waves, when the receiving set being destroyed, they again become undecipherable and are lost in numberless ether vibrations?

In this new problematic theory, the question of the "immortality of the soul," would present itself very differently. One would wonder, for example: Do people make a complete return to universal "psychism?" What intensity of understanding and of love must the perception attain in order to survive apart from the organism, thanks to which it emerged? Or yet again: Under what conditions will the person be able to regain consciousness in a new organism? And if this life is thus a preparation for a new birth, one will have to admit the abortions of souls, doubtlessly, as numerous as abortions of embryos, of which the pediatricians say one out of two die before term.

What would the role of Christ become in this conception? It would no longer be to revive us by a surgery as masterful as our creation but to reveal to us how we ought to live in order that our being will know a hereafter. He initiates us into this life of faith and love which holds the promises and is already the leaven of eternity.

Immortality of the Soul

Christians have believed for a long time that Revelation imposed upon them a belief in the immortality of the soul. Their individual survival is thus guaranteed to them both by the gospel and by Platonic philosophy. But they did not notice that they left to Christ only the glory of resuscitating the body, and that belatedly, at the Final Judgment.

On the other hand, by making of the resurrection a purely spiritual notion, they did not make it very attractive. "An immortality, uniquely spiritual leaves us indifferent," says Guardini. We would find ourselves again in the situation of primitive peoples who believed in an enfeebled, inconsistent, anemic, posthumous state. Homer said: "I would rather live on earth as a slave in the home of a man who possessed no land and of meagre means than to be enthroned among the dead." And he called these "weak heads."

But the philosophy of man has changed; the distinction between matter and spirit becomes difficult when matter is immaterialized into energy, when it is represented by waves, rather than by corpuscles, or by electrons the location of which cannot be determined at a given moment of time. The unity of man has been vigorously affirmed and demonstrated. Think of psychosomatic medical science.

Even theologians are embarrassed by the former concept of the "separated Soul." Until the final resurrection, the soul

remained somewhat suspended in an undefinable and temporary state that was described, however, as very happy, and
the soul would finally recover the body, like an honorary but
cumbersome decoration, from which it had long ago passed.
At the present time, theologians are evolving towards a
thesis, formerly heretical, that the resurrection takes place
immediately at death (Troisfontaines) and Ladislaus Boros
writes in *Concilium* number 60, page 17:

> ...the opinion according to which the soul would exist
> without the body between the moment of death and the
> general resurrection at the end of time — God intervening
> especially to prevent the soul from coming to animate the
> body as is of its nature — appears to me to constitute a bizarre
> notion, logically unsatisfactory and even grotesque.

Resurrection of Bodies

The New Testament uses two vocabularies in speaking of
survival. It speaks of resurrection and it speaks of eternal
life. This double formulation of the same mystery warns us
not to take too literally the more spectacular of them: the
resurrection of bodies.

This ambiguous term suggests that it is not a matter of a
corpse, though Christ's promise concerns the renovation of
the whole person, of all that essentially makes us human,
that is to say, incarnate spirit. It is not your body which will
come to life again, but you, yourself.

It also insinuates an emergence from the grave, hence, a
reanimation of the corpse. Now, a great many modern
theologians admit that their faith in the resurrection of Jesus
would not change if his bones were discovered. Because the
resurrection of Christ is not a return to his former life but an
unimaginable transformation which introduces him into a
totally new human life.

Besides, it supposes that Jesus was resuscitated other than we will be, since our bodies remain in the grave. But the image of Jesus emerging from the tomb has made such a deep impression that the Church for a long time forbade cremation. Our remains must one day also experience this awakening, and in the interest, doubtless, of trying to ease the Lord's work of reconstitution, the Church guarded the bones as intact as possible.

Finally, what a strange idea of God such an image conveys. First he lets us die in anguish, to the distress of our relatives, and then he recreates us by an invisible miracle.

Eternal Life

Jesus speaks of resurrection—the cultural context then obliged it—but he expresses the same reality in other language much better adapted to our times. He promises his disciples that they will never see death. "Whoever lives and believes in me, shall never die" (John 11:26). He introduces them to a life that will have no end: "If any one eats of this bread, he will live forever" (John 6:51).

How do you understand these texts?

Jesus is evidently not affirming that his faithful followers will be exempted from biological death, but he assures them that the life begun in his radiance will not be interrupted by death.

Many Christians interpret these words as the promise of a reward, the announcement of a divine intervention in favor of those who merit it. But eternal life is not a *future* reward. If it is eternal, it exists from today on.

Such is surely the thinking of Jesus: one has access to this life by an immediate conversion and one chooses it by comparison and experience.

Experience of life: "I am the resurrection and the life; he

who believes in me, though he die, yet shall he live, and whoever lives and believes in me shall never die" (John 11:25).

Test of action: "If any man's will is to do his will, he shall know whether the teaching is from God or whether I speak on my own authority" (John 7:17).

Test of liberty: "If you continue in my word...you will know the truth, and the truth will make you free" (John 8:31-2).

Experience of happiness: "If you know these things, blessed are you if you do them" (John 13:17).

Test of brotherly love: Who is my neighbor? He who needs you! (Luke 10:30-37)

Test of fruitfulness: "And every one who has left houses or brothers or sisters...for my name's sake, will receive a hundredfold and inherit eternal life" (Matthew 19:30). "But whoever drinks of the water that I shall give him will never thirst; the water that I shall give him will become in him a spring of water welling up into eternal life" (John 4:14).

This realism is more persuasive than a promise concerning a future life. Basically, Jesus reveals to us that a life of love and of faith is *of itself* eternal.

Already the poets have told us that love is not a moment of oblivion which anticipates death but that it opens a window onto eternity. Already lovers promise each other an eternal love (if you only love yourself in this life, you do not love yourself). Long before now, the Old Testament has sung of love as strong as death, and that it is worth more than the sacrifice of all goods (Canticle of Canticles, 8:6-7).

Jesus confirms the premonition that there exists from this earth on a life by which one can live forever and for which it is worth dying, a life, that the physical universe can neither give nor take away, because it is formed by the spiritual efforts of the one who has chosen it.

Jesus has not brought this life from heaven; it is not a

"supernatural" force which did not exist before him. It has always resided in each person, because nothing is more human (and more rare) than to love. This aspiration towards a personal and universal love, Jesus lived. Jesus accomplished it in an exceptional manner, and thus revealed to us the truth about our own humanity.

A Christian, then, neither lives nor dies, nor does he "rise" otherwise than the rest of humanity. He endeavors to be only as fully human as he is able to be.

This life is *naturally* immortal if God is love, because a life of love is a participation in his being. Let one believe or not believe in God, let one be Christian or not, everyone can live by love and make an experiment of it. They may call it "a true life," or a "supreme value," or the "final foundation," it matters little. They will all act as if this kind of life introduced them into an authentic existence, as if it defied death, as if it far surpassed all other human values and was worth all sacrifices, even that of the earthly life.

In this manner, we will not surmise or conjecture the existence of a beyond *after* death but establish *in ourselves* the presence of a hereafter from this life on. It is our present life which admits of a hereafter, from its appearances, from its mysterious dimension to be indefinitely explored, from the mystery of faith, of hope and of love which convinces us that our reality does not exhaust itself in this present biological existence.

In our experience of life, we possess the wherewithal to brave death.

Purgatory and Reincarnation

The common idea of Purgatory shocks good sense. How could the God of Jesus Christ impose chastisements and expiations?

But on the other hand when one observes people how can one believe that their destiny is irreparably determined by the moment, so perilous, of their death? Are we not tempted by the example of other religions to imagine a new trial, a time of reorientation?

From this point of view, Purgatory is at the same time too much and too little: too little, since the final fate is nevertheless already decided; too much, since these sufferings are powerless to change our destiny.

One would prefer a metempsychosis (reincarnation, transmigration) which would give to each person some chance to do better, if one did not stumble against the inevitable objection: what good is it to recommence an existence if one does not remember the former one? In reincarnation one starts from scratch, one does not carry over the earlier life. Multiply transmigrations as much as you please, new manifestation will be as if another being were born rather than an assurance of progress over a previous existence. When the roulette wheel rolls to a stop, nothing guarantees that it will be on a better number than the first time. And which identity will the person have preserved through the metamorphoses?

The decisive response is doubtless, that of psychoanalysis. Transmigration is suggested to us by the well-known phenomenon of false recognition. We have all lived those strange moments when one experiences again an inexplainable impression of "déjà vu"; where one wavers between two levels, that of real life and that of another life which one thinks one recognizes without being able to identify it.

Spontaneously, we are tempted to attribute them to the memory of a previous existence but psychoanalysis explains them as the happenings which have inscribed themselves on our subconscious minds in the course of infancy and which return to us as if from another world.

Bergson proposes a slightly different explanation. Our memory registers, without our knowledge, all the impressions which come to us. Only a small number of these penetrate our consciousness. Now, it has happened occasionally that we become conscious of this recording of impressions by the memory. They seem, therefore, to come from the past, since we receive them from the memory, whereas they correspond to a present situation. One proof of this theory, is that we constantly think ourselves on the point of guessing what is going to follow, as would be natural if it truly concerned the past and yet we are incapable of doing it. It concerns, then, a registering of the present which takes the disguise of the past.

To do justice to what all these hypotheses of "new possibility" have in common, I would rather insist on the exceptional importance of the "moment" of death.

We are ignorant of what happens after death, and we have based our reflections on what precedes it. But an interval remains: the very act of dying.

No one can evaluate the duration of it. Our forefathers thought that the spirit did not leave the body at the moment of apparent death. Whence those funeral wakes, those ceremonies, that space of three days after which death was considered definite.

In our day, since the progress in the technique of reanimation, the doctors hesitate to define "real" death. At any rate, we will be buried with a good number of our cells still alive. It took us nine months to be born, how much time will we take to die? And how long, if there is survival, for us to adapt to the new condition?

But the duration matters little. Psychological time is not clock time. A very short time can be so filled with events that it seems to last a lifetime. Many people, in mortal danger, have reviewed, in an instant, their whole existence with details which they thought they were unable to remember. "Does pain last . . . a long time?" asks the priest who is going to be shot, in Graham Greene's novel, *The Power and the Glory*. "No, no, it is a matter of a second," answers the lieutenant. "And how long does a second last?"

In this interval we see the occasion for a new decision. Some people perceive it as the moment of the reincarnation, or of that perfecting, which is awaited from Purgatory.[1]

Man, stripped of his possessions and of his diversions, called upon to orient himself toward a final destiny, more conscious than ever of his essential need for Good and Truth, is he not in an immensely stronger position to choose his eternity?

And children who die before the age of reason, the mentally handicapped, the insane, will they not acquire, at that moment when the tyranny of their deficient organisms relax, the possibility of choosing?

"Surrender your soul," according to the popular expression, is it not an invitation to commit yourself utterly into the hands of others?

"Pray for the dead" is not an effort to render God more favorable to them than he is but to think of them with love, to assist them in this passing during that decisive and doubtlessly sorrowful transition. The Mass for the Dead ought to be a service of communion, of sharing.

And even further, are the dead not continuing to be bound up with the evolution of humanity, are they not participating in its progress? Are not the hazards of the date and place of birth compensated by a participation in the discoveries of the more favored?

If this were true, we would not only be responsible for the living but we would also be entrusted with bringing the dead, little by little, to the light of the true life. That which is saddest in our bereavement, is it not our inability to do something for those we love so much? What a comfort to think that we are remaining interdependent with them and that they are sharing in each step we take towards light and towards love.

Heaven

The image of heaven which Catholicism presents to us does not fill anyone with desire to go there. The "eternal rest," the motionless contemplation of the divine perfection, the celestial liturgy where we never cease singing and praising God, all of this is more a bugbear than a promise.

We need, at the same time, both time and eternity, the relative and the absolute. Without eternity we are without direction and without time we are without movement and without life. We wish to participate in the life of God but not to dissolve into him, because if our death restores us totally to our Creator it is as if there had never been a creation. We will add nothing to infinity and infinity will bring us nothing, if we are no longer conscious of being ourselves.[2]

The only perfection for imperfect beings is in their improving themselves endlessly. The only thing which responds in a finite being to boundless divine perfection is a limitless perfectibility. Nothing is more unbearable for an imperfect creature than immobility. We need an active, progressive, inventive heaven where our human faculties find full employment.

Between time, such as we know it, and God's eternity (forever inaccessible to us), philosophy conceives a duration which is not, like time, the measure of local movement, but a succession of spiritual acts. The notion of creature necessarily implies, so it seems, the temporality of the species.

Is it not simplistic, moreover, to suppose that it suffices to die in order for everything to change; and will there not be a long adaptation to this new condition, and then an endless development?

If eternal life is essentially love, love of God and love of others, who can envision it as a rest? The "repose of the warrior" is better assigned to hell. Man will always be unfulfilled, but his happiness will consist in being perpetually en route to completion.

Hell

It excites the greatest incredulity. However hell seems absolutely justified since it expresses God's respect for human freedom. God will never compel anyone to love him. If one does not tolerate the presence of God, he must be able to go elsewhere.

But this final failure of God and of our human community is impossible to accept. Will we be happy if our beatitude coexists with the damnation of our brothers and sisters?

I see only one response. So many men destroy themselves completely during their lives, they shut themselves up, through fear, egoism, and laziness, behind boundaries that are more and more narrow. They dissipate themselves in pleasures and in superficial interests. Hell would complete this movement of weakening, of waste of self by a kind of progressive disintegration. Finally there would be nothing left of them to love. Literally, they would withdraw themselves from our affection. When a person, in spite of our appeals, has exercised his will for licentiousness until the end, what will remain of him to prompt our compassion?

No one can know if some humans reach this degree of negation, but does not each one of us guess, at certain moments, that there is in us the possibility and even relish for that hell?

Conclusion

Modern man knows that the beyond eludes him completely, that all the positings of religions about an other life are
suspect and often barbarian or infantile and that one must
not risk our single, actual existence for unverifiable legends.

What our contemporaries search for is to live as full a life
as possible. They remain indifferent to "heaven" and the
beyond but they are passionately interested in this world, if
someone offers them a task which is worth the effort it
requires.

If this life and this task must be continued after death, it
will be because of their intrinsic quality and not thanks to any
religious assurances, nor to any revelations favoring the élite,
nor to the intervention of a "Savior." The quality of what one
has lived does not encourage one to no longer live; on the contrary, it urgently imposes the necessity for life's continuance.

This attitude corresponds to a series of impressive,
evangelical affirmations. Christ said that the Kingdom of
God is already present among us. "The Kingdom of God is
not coming with signs to be observed; nor will they say: 'Lo,
here it is!' or 'There!' for behold the kingdom of God is in
you." (Luke 17:20-21) Eternal life is not a future life. One
lives it from this earth and beyond. "And this is eternal life,
that they know Thee, the only true God, and Jesus Christ
whom thou hast sent." (John 17:3)

Thus, it is a matter of living now as one would like to live
always. But it is not so simple that one is able to believe it.
The only life which is eternally livable is a life very different
from our petty, inert, unconscious and selfish existence (to
perpetuate it, would be the worst punishment). It is another
life which a person discovers one day as through a special
grace, which is so intense and so enjoyable that eternity will
not exhaust it.

Herein lies the dividing line between two categories of Christians in this present day.

All have accepted as a charter of their faith, the upsetting revelations of the parable of the Final Judgment in St. Matthew (chapter 25:35): "for I was hungry. . . ." They know that they will be judged on their human relations and not on their religious practices. To recognize God or not is excusable but to recognize or ignore one's neighbor is decisive.

They admit that rectitude of life is always a personal discovery, a surprise, an invention. This life is not assured by rites, nor by obedience to laws, nor by the profession of a credo. Refer to the parable of the sower, the talents, the foolish and wise virgins: you must work according to your insights, to your initiative, without instructions or revelations which would exempt you from your responsibilities.

They will finally understand that religious teaching will always be insufficient, since one must await the Last Judgment in order that believers as well as unbelievers discover that God was made man, that the Word was their neighbor, that the first commandment was practically the second.

But then is posed the divisive question: Does it suffice to know and practise that? Is it sufficient to devote oneself to humanity? Is altruism the first and last word of Christian Revelation? Is policy the whole of man?

No, the gospel goes further than the discovery of human truth. Simple dedication to mankind is a good way, but alone it is not an introduction to the real life. There are, besides, some zeals which are as burdensome and as stifling as exploitations. Attention to others can be the means and the excuse for exempting ourselves from delving into our own truthfulness towards all people and for forgetting the emptiness of our own existence.

In order to be fully faithful to the gospel, it is necessary to understand that all sorts of dedication do not save any more than all kinds of prayers. At the source of these two activities one must accept an enlightenment, one must open oneself to an inspiration, to a grace which renders our presence to others as free, as gracious, as transparent as the "visitation" from which we profited.

For love is in us but, as if it were, not of us. The more we learn to love and the more we realize that love is given to us, the better we will know that it does not belong to us and that the condition for it to grow is that we efface ourselves.

The paradox of man dwells in this: he needs Another, others, to be himself. His best moral, religious and artistic achievements, he receives from elsewhere. His highest virtue is reception. What we need above all else is to cultivate not the will, not the reason, nor science, but the natural capacity for inspiration. Our reason is only the mill which grinds the grain brought in from elsewhere. In many persons the mill turns emptily.

What does it profit a man to gain the whole world if he lose his own soul, if he be cut off from his interior dimension, if he no longer be in communication with his Source?

Christian conversion is not a simple moral change; it is an encounter, a revelation, an interior animation which transforms all existence.

NOTES

[1] The books of Kübler-Ross *(The Last Moments of Life)* and of Raymond Moody *(Life after Life)* confirm, by the remarkable convergence of witnesses, our conception of transition between life and death, and of an account of one's life in a beneficent light.

It remains, that all these people who have endured an apparent death are not truly dead.

[2] More and more Christians, through false humility, accept a merging after death, as do the Buddhists in the Nirvana, in the Absolute of the Being; or, as the Marxists, in the future society, in humanity moving towards happiness. They do not attach enough importance to their little "ego" to require the preservation of it. They agree to lose consciousness of themselves in a universal Conscience.

One might ask them how a conscience can be universal and at the same time be unconscious of individual consciences. But one must go deeper.

With man, the need for identification exists from birth. He retains the nostalgia of the uterine symbiosis, of being completely accepted and taken charge of, of floating in indistinctness, without collisions and without limits.

But this retrogressive ideal is the contrary of love. Love demands differentiation, a dualism which is unceasingly surmounted, unceasingly renascent. Love wants simultaneously itself and the other, itself in the other, and the other within itself. If love is itself, I have not gone out of self, and if it is totally the other, I have not attained love. Loneliness remains. If the other identifies itself with me what remains for me to love? And if I identify myself to the other, who still loves?

The ideal of a fusion is an ideal strange to love. It does not aspire to union, but to unity. Love respects distinctness, love creates and enriches the lovers. True union differentiates while helping each one to become more himself.

It is not differences which form an obstacle to union but the lack of love, the reversion to self, the rejection of the other; a refusal which is the same both in the fusion or in the severance.

The steamroller of human or divine collectivism does not create union. Its unity does not tolerate differences and is incapable of surmounting them. It reduces everything to itself because it ignores the love of the other.

Christianity has understood that people are proportionately more themselves as they love each other more and that they are accordingly more united as they are more animated with intelligence and love.

CHAPTER 4

Contemporary Rationalizations of the Mystery

Formerly, death was natural and familiar. It has become intolerable for our contemporaries.

The explanation is evident. People can no longer accept death because they no longer achieve a superior value in life. Life is for them the supreme good, and if death is total destruction, one understands why they hate it with all their strength.

Scientific and technical evolution stimulate the problem still further. Our methods of work have increased wonderfully. Freed by machines from creating goods, we begin to wonder if it is worth the trouble of using them. Mankind, up to now, has been engrossed in the struggle for life, in the fight against hunger, cold, painful exertion. Today, foreseeing victory, one wonders what it is worth, and with what we can busy ourselves later. As our means become gigantic (they are going so far as to permit a global suicide), the problem of termination becomes more acute. The person who has neither shoes nor bread lives in the hope that things will change when he is provided with them. But the man who is shod and nourished is despondent if he finds no work for his expanded powers.

This despair can go so far as a "sit-down strike" against life, as evidence that it is useless to want to prolong what must, in any case, end. Our contemporaries reveal a weariness,

a "loathing of life," a melancholy which urges them to accept as a diversion even a catastrophe, even an atomic war.
Teilhard de Chardin as early as 1947 pointed out:

> I repeat: despite all appearances, Mankind is bored. Perhaps
> this is the underlying cause of all our troubles. We no longer
> know what to do with ourselves. Hence in social terms the
> disorderly turmoil of individuals pursuing conflicting and
> egoistical aims; and, on the national scale, the chaos of arm-
> ed conflict in which, for want of a better object, the excess of
> accumulated energy is destructively released . . . "Idleness,
> mother of all vices."
>
> Teilhard de Chardin: *The Future of Man,* p. 151

Man has never conquered despair except by faith.
Human life is unjustifiable if it is shut up within itself. All
activity needs a goal, and without an unlimited future, the
aims no longer have goals.

Let us examine the proposals of meaning, that is to say,
the superior values of life which permit one to accept death.
The ultimate significance of death is, doubtless, a demand
for transcendency, a summons to be aware of what is worth
more than life.

Why These Questions?

At the threshold of this inquiry, we are stopped by the objection of the young who say: "Life has a meaning all its
own. It is good to live; it has relish. My life is justified by
what I do and what I feel. I need no confirmation from outside. I live, and that is enough for me."

Here is a refusal to think and to verify. As if it were easy to
know what it is to live when there are so many ways of living
and so many illusions in life. Is there not a better manner of
living than yours? Even political leaders challenge you "to

change your life." But what is the "true life," and what will assure the "quality of life"?

Does not man characterize himself by the questions that he asks about a life where there is no contentment in living? And the problem of death, our own as well as that of others, does it not come up *during* life? Man is future oriented. If he does not reflect upon his life, on his reasons for living and for dying, if he no longer foresees, if he does not know that he is going to die, in what does he differ from an animal?

But there is a truth in the objection. Yes, a life justifies itself from the interior. No sanction nor reward coming from the exterior can change the quality of a life. It is valuable or not because of itself.

Even for a Christian in a life of real charity, God does not add himself. He is within. For "Whoever loves, is born of God and knows God."

Life has a meaning in itself. It is not just its continuation which justifies it. But this meaning, does it not require that it prolong itself, that it open out onto a future? Otherwise, the meaning is so contradicted that life becomes absurd. We spend our existence in forming ourselves into a person, in creating ties which are more and more numerous and deeper, and would death destroy this being and these bonds as if they never existed? Does one love only for a while? Does one work to create things which will then disappear? One of the worst punishments in the concentration camps consisted in making the inmates carry piles of stones from one place to another, and then to carry them back.

Man is future oriented; he is constantly generating projects, and it is these which sustain him in life. He lives more in the future than in the present and the past. If, abruptly, we were to have no more future, if someone informed us that we would learn nothing more, that we would cease creating, that we would love no more, life would become absurd, we would be dead before dying. But should our life end unexpectedly through this absurdity, all that we have lived is contradicted and annulled. Our life loses its meaning, which was to continue.

Metaphysical restlessness does not endure death before all else. It concerns the quality of life. But one decisive proof of this quality is death. What remains of it, and if nothing remains of it, why was it important enough to have existed?

It is useful, even though it is not indispensable, to be aware of what gives us life, of our purpose, of the real reasons which make us act. Freud demonstrated to us that it is not easy, and that the best intentions paved hell.

Most certainly, despite false ideas, a man may conduct himself well and contrarily, one with correct ideas may conduct himself viciously. But the ideal is to unite one's ideas and conduct. For people may be mistaken in their ideas. But ideas do not deceive people: they unavoidably develop their logical consequences. An absurd idea like that of Nazism inspired some admirable self-sacrifices but there was a worm in the fruit. Unrecognized errors become poisonous and the young SS idealist found himself a guard in concentration camps and a supplier of crematory ovens.

We are forced by our natures or by circumstances to interrogate ourselves, to question our spontaneous attitudes. Instincts and feelings are murky torches and it is necessary to recognize what they reveal and what they hide.

And the questions to ask yourself are: Why love? Why sacrifice oneself to others?

He who finds answers feels that he is operating well. Not only is he in agreement with his conscience but especially he perceives that he is in the truth of life, that he is responding to a deep appeal.

But even with this immediate certitude, he would not be human if he did not occasionally doubt it. We cannot admit that truth is definite as it corresponds to our tastes, our temperaments, our moods. Even if we are alone in recognizing truth, we think that it is valuable for all.

Now if nothing surpasses human life in worth, it becomes the supreme reward and one must overturn the ethics which drew its inspiration up to now from a faith we no longer share. This willingness to love and to sacrifice explain themselves for those who think thereby to perpetuate themselves to their highest point. They become literally immoral for those who lose all in forgetting themselves. If everything is finished for us after this life, there is no greater value than our existence. We have the duty to preserve and develop it. We will even practise a generosity capable of expanding us, but not sufficient to urge us to annihilate ourselves.

You sacrifice yourself for reasons of conscience? But just so, you lose perception by sacrificing yourself.

You cannot live as a slave? But you also cease being free by ceasing to exist.

You ennoble yourself by refusing to live in such conditions? But by losing your life, you also lose the dignity attained by your sacrifice.

How can one explain that the sacrifice of self is indispensable for the growth of self, if this sacrifice destroys the "ego" and its expansion? How justify an unconditional love, if the meaning of the universe is not love, but indifference and a game?

Let us question our contemporaries: "Is the essence of reality a kind of impersonal and pitiless Moloch who sacrifices one generation after the other for the beauty of the spectacle of evolution; or rather, a burst of love and of life aspiring to self-revelation by communicating himself?"

It is not secondary, it is not a useless complication to have understood that you have rediscovered unconsciously the

fundamental Christian truth: "God is love," when you
pledged your life to love and dedication.

Man is divided between the horror of death and the impulse to face it. We feel very deeply that our individuality is
inestimable, irreplaceable, and yet we aspire to go beyond it
in order to participate in something greater than self.

We all act as if the reason for living were worth more than
life. But what is your reason for living?

Since the beginning, men have sacrificed themselves, with
a readiness which was often scandalous, for causes which inspired them. They were divided only on the choice of the
value which merited their sacrifice.

Humanity and the Future, False Transcendences and Real Alienations

Nowadays, numerous human beings declare that the
values superior to life are society, humanity and the future.
"The only transcendence of men without God," said Camus,
"is the future." What Christians expect from their God,
many of our contemporaries await from future generations:
a survival—but so pale, so discolored, so ephemeral.

"As for me," one will modestly say, "I have no ambition
for a personal immortality. I do not attach such importance
to my 'ego' as to claim it is important to perpetuate it. The
thought that something of me survives in my children is
enough to content me. I need no other future than theirs
and I feel happy at the idea that, mingled with them, I will
share in their discoveries, in their experiences and in their
joys. I need no other immortality than this communion with
them."

"But," some one will respond, "if this particle of you
which lives in your children is not conscious of you, it is exactly as if there were no part of you in them. You will par-

ticipate in nothing of their lives. This thought satisfies you, yes, as long as you think (and yet, not too far!), as long as you are capable of having a thought, but death is precisely the extinction of all thought. This portion of you in your children will be no different from a share of beefsteak or of beans. In speaking so, you deny the specific characteristic of human nature in comparison to animal or vegetable nature: the capacity for reflective perception. Logically, you ought to lean towards cannibalism. According to your principles, man-eating would assure the survival of our contemporaries in preference to the survival of animals and of plants which we have favored up until now.

And it is very dangerous to want to prolong yourself in your descendants. You will quickly learn that they rebel against this interference. They will cry out with all their might that they do not resemble you (look at their hair, their clothes, their music), that they will not prolong you at all, that they are themselves, not you, and you will find yourselves alone and mortal. "All that we had hoped for, all that we would have wanted, all that we have not succeeded in accomplishing, you will be obliged to do, my little one," said Jacques Thibault to his nephew, as if his values had necessarily become those of his nephew.

"Well and good," will insist the father of a family, "let us abandon this type of immortality as still too individualistic. Why can you not be contented with a continuation of life in humanity, a life which will be more beautiful and happy, thanks to our accomplishments? The human species forms a unity. It is obviously called upon to unite itself constantly more intensively. I do not distinguish my destiny from my neighbor's. I feel myself interdependent and strive only for this survival."

This is the position of the greater number of Marxists. Man, a social being, lives again in the species, if the connections among humans are not alienated and if they thereby assure a complete and reciprocal communication among individuals. Militants and heroes will survive in the mind and hearts of people in their struggles.

And the others?

But people themselves will stop fighting some day, be they conquered or victorious, and they will die like any other individuals. And what will be said of a man who dies very simply in a car accident? It is recounted, that in a discussion on this subject, a communist replied: "In the perfectly organized future society, there will be no more car accidents!"

But above all, what fellowship is there for a person who will not be aware of it? He enjoys it now that he is capable of thinking but what will remain of it, and therefore of him, when he will no longer be there to think of it?

You give yourself for those who surround you? No, you leave them a work, an example, a discovery, but you destroy at the same time the unique value which you constitute for them: yourself. None of your gifts can excel the value of your being. The most precious thing which you possess is not transmissible: your personality. Your gift disappears in the very act through which you try to transmit it.

No one can continue *your* life. Humanity is a deceptive word which seems to give stability to what is essentially fluent, a false totality since it does not sum up the partial totals, a label which is being endlessly attached to other contents, since people die and disappear, whereas Humanity, fictitiously remains.

Will you say that Bach and Mozart die, but that their music continues? No, other musicians will create. They will, perhaps, have been influenced by them, but Bach and Mozart will not continue. They are irreplaceable and unique. The survival of their work is not the survival of its creators. And it is at the mercy of an accident. The music and painting of ancient Greece have almost completely disappeared.

Conferring on humanity a substantial value capable of justifying the death of the people who compose it is to treat the human species like an animal species, and even like a machine with interchangeable cogwheels. It is a self-deception for bringing quantity into a domain where each being is unique and exists, first of all, for itself. It is a dangerous delusion, entailing the immolation of one life for several. "It is proper that an innocent person die for the people." Man will never be more than coal to shovel into the locomotive of history, a raw material to be used according to the convenience of the sociological human group.

May one use man or must one respect in him an incomparable value? Is man at the service of humanity, or is society at the service of human happiness? These are forcefully opportune questions for our Maoist age. "If God does not exist," said Berdiaev, "man is entirely dependent on nature and society, on the world and on the State."

You accept death in times of war or of revolution to liberate your wife and children? But you know perfectly well, that the greatest service to render them would be to save yourself for them, even in a conquered country, or even in an occupied or enslaved one. No, you do it for yourself, because you can not admit slavery and injustice, and you sacrifice even your home with your life, so much do you have faith in a value and a justice which excel them.

"But," you will say, "this value is society's future, for humanity will continue to uplift itself, thanks to the devotedness of its predecessors."

Very well die on the battlefield: "The wheat will be more beautiful. The better the soil the better the crops." Why can you not see that humanity is not, for the individual, merely a temporary state? This humanity will perish one day.

Humanity, like the individuals who compose it, is mortal. Man is not the transcendence of man, and the future is not composed of another material than the present. It is a hopeless enterprise to look for a reason to live in beings who have no more than we have.

The resources of our species, our planet, are not infinite. Our world will spin someday like a dead star, no different from those which have never known life. You deny individual survival, do not invent, in order to delude yourself, a collective survival.

It is, therefore, as ineffectual to want to prolong the life of humanity as that of individuals. Its ultimate fate is the same: perishable.

> The absurdity of the term implies indifference from the starting point. An end, incapable of benefiting from our gifts, is not sufficient to solicit our generosity. Let us suppose that the people of tomorrow prize the sacrifices which we are asked to impose upon ourselves for them. It is then that they will be beyond comparison, more disinterested than ourselves, seeing that each generation will enrich itself by despoiling the preceding generation. So this flow of generosity risks not ending anywhere, in this endowment, always continued, which can be neither justified nor welcomed. Zundel

What must end someday may also end immediately. What will change in the appearance of the galaxies, if humanity has lived or not, if it has existed for a long time or not, if it be happy or unhappy?

And yet, out of pity for your descendants, you ought to spare them the cost of your sacrifices. For the most disheartening thought for the last people, witnesses of the death of the planet, will be precisely that of all the sacrifices by which their predecessors have spoiled their chances of happiness and lost their lives in a fruitless endeavor to prolong and ameliorate theirs.

To promise man vindication for his sacrifice toward a collective good is nonsense. The real "opium of the people," is it not to entice the individual from a "revivification" from which he would benefit, into a future humanity of which he will never be a part? Would it not be clearer and more forthright to declare, once and for all, that each person and each generation is dedicated to total annihilation, that they have or have not contributed to an improvement of the species?

The collectivists rightly fight the present-day alienations, but they make final and worse the alienation from the future, that is to say, the exploitation of the living for the sake of their descendants.

Marx dares to write:

Death appears to be a hard victory of the species over the individual; but the individual is only a generic determined creature, and, as such, mortal. Karl Marx: *Manuscripts of 1844.*

But across this series of victories, the species, too, advances to its defeat and will be conquered by death. Perhaps, the tomorrows will sing, but they will also surely gasp in death.

If man is only a passing instrument of collective destiny, if he must adhere to the hard biological law of renewal and improvement of the species by means of individuals, why not go to the end of this logic of nature, and eliminate the handicapped, allow the strong to devour and exploit the weak, set up in a moral code the stern realities of the struggle for life and for the survival of the fittest?

For him who has no reason to live and to die nowadays, it is vain to await the passing of time and the multiplication of people. If today there is no value which justifies our own existence in itself, there will be none tomorrow. The absolute is not formed by the addition of relative values, nor is a value formed by accumulating zeros. "If a person has no more worth than a fly, twenty billion flies are of the same value — insignificant."

In order to live in peace, a man must know (and he does know it "in the secret depths of his being," says Maritain) that he will live forever. In order to combat with one's whole force, one must recognize a result worthy of the struggle. In order to love as one wants and needs to love, one must realize that love is an immediate participation in the supreme Reality which expresses itself throughout the world. In order to sacrifice oneself unto death, one must believe that love is stronger than death.

The innermost reason for every man at certain moments to feel that he can or ought to die for his brethren, is that he has a presentiment that such a love does not perish. It is because he experiences, in thus dying, a state invulnerable to time and to evil, which is more than a promise, which is the substance and the very taste of eternity.

Moreover, it is not the future society, which the Marxists believe is the object of their dedication, but it is the values of generosity, of truth and of justice which they affirm in sacrificing themselves. The philosopher Kolakowski declares:

> We are not communists because we consider the future of communism as a historic necessity. We are communists because we are for the oppressed, against the oppressor, for the poor against their masters, for the persecuted against their persecutors. Every practical choice is a choice of values, a moral choice. Quoted from Fejto: *Histoire des Démocraties populaires* II, 104.

Were it true that if the future society ceased respecting these values, society would have interest in them no longer.

They would protect the individuals maltreated by that society, and would prefer that society perish rather than triumph unjustly.

Even without a future, even if humanity ought to perish tomorrow, I am persuaded that generous unbelievers would not stop, against all their logic, to work, to love, and to dedicate themselves. Their life goes beyond their motivation.

Death is a personal problem. One does not exonerate it by transferring it to others.

Nonmortality

There are those who believe that before long they can escape the problem of dying. They foresee that science will succeed in conquering death.

Already, one envisages the refrigeration of incurable invalids who will be thawed when the remedy will have been discovered. But, in fact, all of the dying are temporary incurable invalids. If they were to await the progress of medicine, of surgery, of gerontology, they would go back to their activities and live interminably. Certain bacteria have been revived after hundreds of million years of dehydration.

In ideal conditions of excretion and of nourishment, there is no reason for tissue to degenerate.[1] The fragment of chicken heart maintained in a laboratory by Carrel was practically immortal. The protozoans reproduced by fission persist endlessly. And do we not have in us, in our genital cells, something of Adam?

When a skillful graft provides us with a kidney, a lung, a liver, an artificial heart miniaturized and indefinitely replaceable, why should we die?

Indeed, these advances are not for tomorrow and one still doubts if science will be capable of keeping organisms alive indefinitely, as they have done for groups of cells. Up to now, man is immortal only in detached pieces.

The most serious scientists foresee a life span of one hundred twenty years as normal for a human being but they do not deny the possibility of someday maintaining life indefinitely.

These perspectives rejoice many atheists and frighten many deists who wonder if they will still believe in God when they shall no longer die.

But what a sorry faith to believe in God through fear of death. Is death the sole motive for believing in God, the only Transcendence which compels a person to excel?

No, the more powerful man is, the longer he lives, the more he will need love. Perhaps, it would even be necessary to admit that death exempts humanity from getting along and loving each other: they do not sufficiently take to heart a temporary existence. When they will know that they can live forever, it will be worth the trouble to understand one another.

We do not need God for dying, but we do to live, to love, to believe that one is right in loving, always and in all circumstances, in order completely to justify our enthusiasm for love and our joy in loving.

For Christians, death is not a decree or a chastisement of God that it would be sacrilegious to transgress, it is simply a problem of human possibility.

But the real question remains: Will man tolerate an indefinitely prolonged existence? Life is unsatisfying, not because it is short but because it never matches our deep aspirations. An unlimited life is not necessarily a different life. Will you never be tired of it? Would it not be a punishment to eternalize an existence incapable of fulfilling us? "Neither the immensity of space, nor the indefiniteness of time can satisfy the infinity of the soul." (Thibon) A more difficult thing to bear than death is our finiteness.

Man will die by choice, through a desire to transcend this world. His most fundamental impulse is to give himself, to offer himself, to throw himself out of self, and even, beyond this crepuscular and unsatisfying world, toward another existence.

Let us measure how primitive and blind we still are to our deep-seated identity, by establishing our difficulty in imagining a person who relishes life, who esteems and blesses it for all that it has brought him and who, however, desires to pass from this manner of existence to another of which this life has given him a foretaste.

Let us add, that in the end, immortality does not differ so much from the classic conception of a life beyond death. It would bring, in effect, so many transformations — physical, biological, mental, social, that it would be a question of a new person, a transformed person. The foretold "revolution" would become then very similar to the old "resurrection," to the traditional hope of emigrating into another life with our better qualities.

There would remain two important differences. The billions of dead before this revolution would naturally not benefit from it. On the contrary, since it has no moral character, it would involve all people living at the moment of this mutation. One is doubtless no more exhilarating than the other . . .

Biological Submission

Then there are others who treat this important mystery lightly. Death, they tell themselves, is a necessity of life. In order for life to be diversified, to improve, the generations must succeed each other. Barois, in full health, states:

Why fear death? Is it different from life? Our existence is

only a ceaseless passage from one state to another: death is
only one more change. Why fear it? What is there so for-
midable in ceasing to be this *whole* — momentarily coor-
dinated — that we are? How can one be so frightened of a
restoration of our elements to an inorganic habitat, since it
is, at the same time, an assured return to unconsciousness?

For me, since I have understood the nothingness which
awaits me, the problem of death no longer exists. I experience even... pleasure... in thinking that my personality
is not lasting... And the certitude that my life is limited...
singularly increases the enjoyment that I take in it...

A few years later, consumed by tuberculosis, he reread
these assertions. "He let the book fall from his knees. He was
crushed by what he had dared to write, formerly, *without
knowing...*"

These considerations confuse sociology with zoology and
dauntlessly extend to the human species what is proper to
animal species where the individual animal is entirely at the
service of the group. But man is defined by the irreducibility
of the individual to the species, by the superiority of the person over society. And moreover, what usefulness for the
species was the death of Einstein or of Michelangelo?

Despair

We much prefer those who brave death without dreaming
about an illusive survival, but also without concealing from
themselves the absurdity to which this lucidity condemns
life.

Jean Rostand remains the example of this tragic honesty:

The mocking atom lost in an inert and enormous cosmos,
man knows that his feverish activity is a petty, local
phenomenon, without significance and without aim. He
knows that his values are only valuable to him, and that,

from a sidereal point of view, the fall of an empire or even the ruin of an ideal does not count more than the collapse of an anthill under the foot of a heedless passerby. Too, fiercely turned in upon himself, he devotes himself humbly, prosaically, to the realization of his puny designs where he will feign to lend the same seriousness as if he were aiming at eternal goals.

We are, on one point, of Rostand's opinion. To *take seriously* our enterprises of creation, of love and of fraternity, it is necessary, in a certain way, to believe them *eternal*. Without future, there is no more present, because man is *much more* in his projects *than in* his actions. Some Americans committed suicide on hearing the famous broadcast by Orson Welles on the invasion by Martians. They preferred to die immediately rather than live without a future.

But who is able, at the same time, to pretend *and* to take seriously? Is it the adult who plays with the child and who is caught up with the game? It is not a solution to the problem of life. One rejects faith and then putters around on a prosthesis of faith which permits one to live.

The true response to Jean Rostand, is it not that of Antigone to Creon? He proves to her, with all the prestige of authority and experience, the absurdity of her beliefs and the futility of life. He easily destroys her illusions and her ideal. Antigone is incapable of refuting his arguments but she dies for her ideals. She flees this uninhabitable universe which projects to her no value worthy of her aspirations. She demonstrates Transcendence by going beyond life.

Bertrand Russell is of the same opinion as Rostand:

> Let man be the product of causes which never had in view the purpose of their efforts. Let his origin, his development, his hopes and his terrors be only the result of accidental collisions of atoms. Let neither fire, nor heroism, nor intensity of thought or feeling prolong an individual life beyond the

grave. May all the labors of the centuries, all the devotion, all the inspiration, all the dazzling renown of human genius be destined to extinguish itself in the vast death of the solar system, and may the whole temple of the work of man inevitably be obliged to be buried under the debris of a universe in ruins. All these things, even if one were able to discuss them, are however, the expression of a truth so near certitude that if truth denied them no philosophy might hope to live.

We think that, if he acknowledges it, no philosopher has reason to live, and that the philosophies which make life impossible do not have much hope for perpetuity.

If, someday, all will be annihilated, why continue to work, to suffer, to procreate? All is equal if all is in vain. All is senseless if there be no direction, no completion, no benefit.

Having lost the reasons to live is being *already* dead. Such thinkers kill themselves immediately in order not to face uncertainty and the anguish of a distressing and unavoidable question. Then, they find subterfuges in order to live, nevertheless, as amputees.

Of course, these considerations are decisive in order to destroy the false promises of either collective or individual immortality. They force the question of survival there where it, in truth, lies: in the presence, within the interior of man, of another sort of life than the biological one.

Let us reread, by contrast, these wholesome words of Teilhard de Chardin:

> There is no virtue in sacrifice when no higher interest is at stake. A universe which would continue *to act laboriously* in the conscious expectation of absolute death would be a stupid world, a spiritual monstrosity, in fact a chimera. Now since in fact the world appears before us here and now as one huge action perpetually taking place with formidable

assurance, there can be no doubt at all that it is capable of nourishing indefinitely in its offspring an appetite for life, which is continually growing more critical, exacting and refined. It must carry within it the guarantees of ultimate success. From the moment that it admits thought, a universe can no longer be simply temporary or of limited evolution: it must by its very structure emerge into the absolute.

And his criticism of Jeans:

There can be nothing more typical or more distressing than the description offered by the great English astronomer Sir James Jeans, in his last and widely read book, *The Universe around Us,* of the future state of the world in "a million million years"; a humanity presumed to be like ours growing old without hope of any morrow on an earth without peaks or mysteries. Jeans offers us this prospect as a "hope," since we have still a long life in front of us (as if our appetite for life, faced by *absolute and certain death,* would find any difference between one year and a million million!). Strange that he can have so little understood both the human spirit's reserves of power and its requirements.

Teilhard de Chardin: "The Spirit of the Earth," *Human Energy,* p. 41

NOTE

[1] Some recent discoveries contradict this affirmation: cellular aging is inevitable.

CHAPTER 5

Fear of Death

Death has terrified me since I learned that I was mortal.
Simone de Beauvoir
La Force de L'âge (The Prime of Life), p. 615

If our contemporaries can no longer confront death, it is because they have lost the taste for and meaning of life. They are divided between the boredom of living and the fear of dying.

Most certainly, this is legitimate and that person who does not experience it deserves to be alarmed. One could suspect such a one of unconsciousness (it would be terrible to die through childishness, through defiance, or out of spite) or, worse still, from inhumanity. The gangster exposes himself voluntarily to death because he is not obliged to anything, nor to anyone. He has no bonds. For us, there are the ties which make us exist, the people who sustain us in life.

I remember my surprise, in the war, I was very young, very idealistic, very "mystic," and I regarded with stupefaction all those men who were afraid, who trembled, who took cover, who sought refuge from the bombs, even under the stretchers of the wounded in hospital trains. Half disgusted, half amused, I used to say to myself: "How can they cling so to life? It has not been merciful to them; they are poor, frustrated, without future or horizon. Why are they so afraid of dying?"

Then, I looked within myself: "You are not attached to anything, you have no capacity to be 'courageous.' You are of an inhuman indifference. These beings are superior to you. They hold on to life, they judge it good in spite of its hardships. They love their wives, their children, their poor joys. One does not attach oneself to life because of what it does for one but because of what one does for life. By dint of working, they love their work. By force of living together, they attach themselves to one another. By force of living they come to the point of loving life."

I felt then that I would not die. I was not worthy of dying, I still had everything to learn of life; to love it first of all, and then to go beyond it.

I no longer esteem those who profess a kind of biological submission to the necessity of dying, as if man fully shared nature where all must die to be reborn, as if the individual must efface itself to benefit the continuation of the species. Instead of clinging to what one suffers, instead of identifying oneself with the animal which dies in us, I prefer rebellion which marks the distance between what happens in us in spite of ourselves and what we are in reality, between what death does to us and what within us braves it and surpasses it. I find the attitude of Jesus in face of death much more human ("my soul is mortally sad. . .with great cries and tears, he implored and supplicated him who was able to save him from death. . ."), in face of this relentless rupture with all one loves, before this loss of consciousness which characterizes the "me." For in all of nature, only man dies.

Animals and plants only exchange their calories, their atoms and their molecules. Their basic material is imperishable. They are constantly being reborn in other plants and other animals which replace them to advantage. "If the grain does not die. . .?" But the grain in the earth does not die. On the contrary, it fructifies, it is the seat of an intense activity, it transforms and multiplies itself. And just so our dead bodies. . .

But man, that is to say, the reflecting conscience, this "I" who resembles no other and whom nothing will replace, this knot of human relations which he has used his whole life in creating and deepening, he, man, is the only being who dies, who disappears without anything apparent continuing to live of what constituted his very self, who is extinguished without compensation, in the universe.

If humanity were only a zoological species like the others, we would accept the law of life which in order to avoid over-population, and in order that the species renew and diversify itself, wants the old to give place to the young and the strong to devour the weak. But our law is wholly different, and it would be better that humanity disappear if we adopted that "natural" law. And moreover, what profit does humanity draw from the death of an Einstein, of a Bach, of a Francis of Assisi, and even of a simple human being whom one has learned to understand and to love?

But the real fear of death is the fear of being lost, fear of the unknown and the fear of separation — let us attempt to meet it.

Fear of Being Lost

We are constantly being divided between the fear and the fascination of death, between the desire to preserve ourselves, and that of giving ourselves, between the desire to establish ourselves, to arrest time and life (which is to be already a dead person, the worst of corpses) and that of risking ourselves, of surpassing ourselves, of experiencing what we have never known — that which invites us to another kind of death.

The ambivalence of adolescence remains into maturity and even until old age. The adolescent wishes to live inexhaustibly but the moment he experiences a contradiction he wishes to die immediately. He aspires to love but dreads giving himself ("for, when he has given himself, he no longer has himself"). He wants to win a great deal immediately and is prepared to renounce it all.

Basically, we are inexorably condemned to lose ourselves. We have only the choice between a sure, immediate, and futile loss, in holding on to our acquisitions "He who wants (too much) to save his life, will lose it." Or we can opt for a risk, a chance of saving ourselves while losing ourselves, of opening ourselves to the unknown, of getting support from what we have experienced of love and of life in order to rely on them for what they still hold for us. Thus refusing to die is, finally, refusing to live, since life always draws us beyond what it has already revealed to us.

That is why Christian faith in eternal life does not at all identify itself with a recovery of the present life, a simple continuation of the past. One must agree "to lose one's life," one must be born to a life as different from ours as postnatal life differs from uterine life — with, however, a continuity of the person in the unforeseeable mutation of life forms.

Fear of the Unknown

Is it not shocking to think, that for all the centuries that there have been people and that they have died, mankind has never come to know what in truth, death is. Is it an annihilation or a birth, a disappearance or an absence? The sphinx which each one meets on his way pitilessly guards the secret of its riddle. Even science, in spite of its extraordinary progress, has not advanced one step in the knowledge of death. No one has ever gone to the other side and returned to instruct us. Even the disclosures of reanimated persons are no revelation as to real death.

Christ spoke to us of life, of personal and community conversion to be accomplished now. But he did not describe the hereafter, except in the conventional phrases of his time: a banquet, a wedding, a new-wine feast, payments in silver (the talents), or in cities, or the "bosom of Abraham." Truly, nothing to excite our imaginations.

One must admit the mystery. We are incapable of making for ourselves any representation of life beyond the tomb — we only know this life.

The whole question is: Is there not within us, from this very moment, the experience of a life independent of death, a seed of eternity? Have we not lived in art, in love, or in prayer, moments which open for us a new dimension of existence, during which we rise out of time, we attain an unbelievable freedom, we experience satisfying moments which could last forever?

These periods pass of course but there remains in us the revelation of a faculty that we rarely exercise, of a strange capacity to reach a state which for us is, at the same time, the most personal and the most unknown. Therein, we understand why our present life does not fulfill us. It is as if we were made for other things. We are secretly possessed by a need and, it must be said, by a certain presence of an absolute against which we measure everything that we live. We have intuitions of the beauty which renders us capable of loving it for itself and of consecrating to it joyfully an ephemeral life, in the same way that our power to love gives us the ability to sacrifice our lives willingly to a value which we are sometimes certain infinitely exceeds the sacrifice.

The only way to inform ourselves about life beyond, is to explore the dimension of this life which requires a going beyond itself.

"Eternal life," says St. John, "is for you to know, the one true God." But he adds: "Whoever loves is born of God and knows God." There is then from this life on, a participation in the absolute, an experience of eternity, offered to each one of us through its deepest appeal, to love and be loved.

Have we not all experienced happiness in instances of intense communication with others? Have we not caught a glimpse of freedom from our loneliness, our selfishness, our inconsistencies; this power which possesses the love to revive the dead, to make us pass from an insensible life to a living life? Love, the real love, is lived as if it would endure forever. It alone renders one capable of eternity, for an eternal life without love is a threat much more than a promise.

Faith and hope will pass, but "Love never ends." (I Cor. 13:8) Nothing will live on in us except our relations of love, our capacity to love. A life of love is a life where God manifests himself, and when I speak of God, I mean what each one esteems in his inner depth as of prime importance, what gives meaning to life, what is worth the sacrifice.

Death frightens us because it precipitates us into an unknown world. But God and eternal life are neither more nor less known to us than love. When God is perceived (rarely) in the texture of daily living, those who recognize love say "God is there" but those who are ignorant of it say "I have never known anything like that. I could live from it forever and for it I could die immediately." And so, when you have an experience of love, you say exactly the same thing.

But God, life, love are not to be comprehended but to be lived and in living them they disclose and justify themselves. We are not asked to believe in it, but to practise it. Have you had the feeling of an extraordinary power of revival, of transformation, of vitalization and of a resurrection coming from love?

Alas! in general, we claim to believe in all of that without having experienced it, without having gone through the act which would establish faith, without our having ventured into the "unknown."

Christ, the great proof of this liberating power, gave it in the multiplication of loaves. He renewed the miracle of the Manna. He asserted himself as a new Moses who delivers a people from oppressors and hunger. The Apostles, like us, took a long time to understand: "And being aware of it, Jesus said to them, 'Why do you discuss the fact that you have no bread? Do you not yet perceive or understand? Are your hearts hardened? Having eyes do you not see, and having ears do you not hear? And do you not remember? When I broke the five loaves for the five thousand, how many baskets full of broken pieces did you take up?' And they said to him, 'Twelve.' 'And the seven for the four thousand, how many baskets full of broken pieces did you take up?' And they said to him, 'Seven.' And he said to them, 'Do you not yet understand?' " (Mark 8:17–21).

If we want, as Peter finally did, to say to Jesus: "You are the Christ," we must make present the messianic sign which occurred to convince Peter: the satisfying of the poor, not only "believe" in the multiplication of loaves but bring about a multiplication of his bread; experience that, from the moment when one brings out bread, or when one risks his own sustenance (seven for four thousand men), there is produced a contagion, a passing on, an infinite fructification.

Have you begun an undertaking which appeared visionary, unrealizable, Utopian but which after humble beginnings, has spread immensely, has won over the skeptics, has persuaded the recalcitrants? When you discover that you are capable of multiplying loaves, when you are a witness to the extraordinary fruitfulness of love, you will know why living and dying are worth while, why one can have confidence in life and in death. You will know that there is an unlimited force hidden in the false life, in the death in which we all live so feebly.

Among us, too often, the blind remain blind, the deaf re-

main deaf, the poor remain poor, and the dead remain
dead. A sign is needed to show that there exists a power
capable of overcoming this death. And if you do not experience it right now, how can you believe in it later?

Has no one ever revived you? Has no one ever spoken to
you, forgiven you, loved you enough to bring you to life
again? Have you never attended resurrections? Have you
never resurrected anyone? Have you experienced the power
of life which bursts forth from a smile, from a pardon, from
a welcome, from a real community? How can you believe in
a future resurrection if you have never felt immediate resurrections? How can you believe that love is stronger than
death if it has not made you alive, if it has not revived you
from death?

Fear of Separation

How explain and how justify, if one is a Christian, this absolute separation between the dead and the living? Why the
"communion of saints" or simply, the communication of
those who love each other, is it so transient and evasive?
Why, if love is stronger than death, is it hindered by death
from manifesting itself? This "great abyss," of which
Abraham speaks in the parable of Lazarus and the wicked
rich man, "established in order that those who would like to
pass from here to you can not, and that they neither may
cross over from down there to us" is a merciless invention
and one which is even more revolting when one admits a
merciful Redemption. How can a good God, after having
launched us so unprotected and blind into an indifferent
world, permit the rending of bonds which we had woven as
our sole protection against solitude? Death has so much
scandalized religious people that they have made of it the
consequence of human sin, rather than accepting it to be

the fault of God. But death is the law of creation!

The experience of solitude in death is terrible "each person dies alone," and one endures it to the point that the only commonplace solace is that of a presence at our side, of a hand which presses ours. At the moment of losing all our ties, as at the moment of birth, a person reassures himself again at the source of a living person.

We live only through our relations; our ties keep us alive. Others maintain us in life if they love us, if they value us, and their absence or their forgetfulness make us die. Death is the worst of absences.

What is there to reply? What recourse is there against these accusations and these complaints?

For most of us, there is that about our dead that there is about God; we address to each the same reproaches and we resign ourselves to the same remoteness. We accuse them of being absent, silent, distant. The absence of God, the silence of God are great themes of contemporary literature along with the lack of communication already existing among the living.

And meanwhile, are there not hours in which God becomes awesomely present? And are there not moments when one feels oneself very sharply near to someone one has loved and thought gone forever? For we are tempted to believe only in a carnal presence. Still, however, we know ourselves to be much more present to those whom we love, even during their absence, than to those whom we elbow in the subway. Above all, we enclose ourselves in our sadness, we believe that it will uplift us, ennoble us, and that our loyalty is well expressed in our despair. Nothing is more false. Sadness is naturally selfish. It measures our attachment to ourselves and our insensibility to others.

The great danger of separation from our dead rests perhaps in our withdrawing into ourselves to avoid suffering too much. We think that we must renounce our dead forever. We cut ourselves off from them as much by our forlornness as by their absence. We concentrate on our pain and by our refusal to keep open the communication with them. It is as if we were banishing them from our life, as if we were silencing them a second time.

Thus, one is forced to think of God no longer because he seems too far away, because he has disappointed us too much, because prayer is too troublesome or in vain.

But if we sincerely consulted those whom we have loved, would we remain locked in our sadness? True loyalty to our deceased is for us to conduct ourselves as they would wish, as they wished while they lived. Is it not by a perverse choice that you close yourself up in your grief, through preference for a painful satisfaction? A father of the Church has said: "There is only one way to cure sadness, and that is by not loving it."

Jesus admirably intimates that in St. John: "And now that I am going away... none of you asks me: 'Where are you going?' but because I have told you these things, sadness has invaded your heart... Yet, if you loved me, you would rejoice that I am going to my Father."

Instead of being interested in him, each disciple only thinks of himself and of the measure of his loss; for no one is enough interested in him to follow him into the beginning of his joy. So it is with our deceased, we are desolate at their loss and indifferent to their fate.

And meanwhile, if we would dare to face the fact that we are no more cut off from our dead than we are from God (he is generally very distant, but sometimes so close), or from love (which at times is very foreign to us, but which we immediately recognize when it happens), or from our better selves (from which we are habitually separated, but towards which we always unconsciously aspire)? If the only contact with the dead were that which we have with life, with love, with joy, with our better selves and with others?

Being dead, is to live only in the essential sense, that is from love, from faith, from hope. But we, the supposed living, we are capable of being entirely taken up with entertainment, with the exterior, with the secondary. (Stupidity is a keen sense of the unessential.)

Those who live only outwardly, risk dying completely, risk exteriorizing themselves, disintegrating themselves indefinitely. It is offered to all of us to live essentially, faithfully and lovingly. And if we have experienced such a choice and it has made us alive, even after the worst changes, we will not refuse to believe that it will keep us living forever and that it will make us closer and closer to those who are already living eternally.[1]

NOTE

[1] Can this proximity be conscious?

Be on guard against the temptation to preserve the old forms of our relations with the dead: surrounding ourselves with souvenirs of them and their photographs, not changing anything in the house, visiting the cemetery regularly.

This false loyalty prevents us from attaining a new kind of presence. Certain people have very lively impressions of this closeness, of beneficial interventions, they feel as if they were inhabited by those they love. Others suffer from an absence and from an unmerciful silence.

The experiences of the spiritualists leave us perplexed and unsatisfied. Vercors explains clearly their apparent results by the fact that all which is cherished imbues and transforms us. Under the effects of a particularly intense emotion, a dialogue can seem to be established between us and the loved one, in so much that the loved one can continue to live and be developed in that part of us which has become theirs. Although we understand the wretchedness of spiritualistic revelations; what we learn from them about the hereafter never exceeds what our weak imagination is capable of conceiving.

At best we can only remain available to them, keep a place for them in our lives, be attentive to welcome signs from them. Above all, after a period of retreat, of painful transformation, our loyalty ought to keep us living and loving and engaged in pursuing the life plans which we began with them. Then will be born that appeasement, that recollection, where little by little, they will become again for us that which they should never have ceased to be, close, loving, comforting.

CHAPTER 6

Suicide and Euthanasia

People assume so many obligations towards life that
they reach a time, when, discouraged of ever being
able to perform them all, they turn towards the graves,
and call upon death, death which comes to assist the
destinies which have difficulty in being accomplished.
Marcel Proust: Les Plaisirs et les Jours
(Pleasures and Days and Other Writings)

Just as he is the only being who truly dies (chapter 5), man is the only being who kills himself solitarily.[1] Lemmings, marmots drown themselves in hordes when their species multiplies to excess. But man withholds this strange power to destroy himself cold bloodedly; when he wishes it, because he wishes it.

The motives for suicide are numerous but the deep-seated reason for this human privilege is always the same. One commits suicide because he has such an esteem of true living that he can no longer endure his life.

Common opinion considers suicide as cowardice but fails to recognize its essential import: a crushing comparison between our being and our existence, a vertiginous imbalance between our infinite desires and our so mediocre realizations, the vanity of wanting to satisfy our aspirations to live without end, in a life always drawing closer to death.

Our life is so different from the "true life" that the platform of all political parties is to "change life." But is it not madness to plan on a change of institutions in order to change the quality of life, or to await from another man, or from circumstances what we ought to invent for ourselves, day after day, without ever definitely attaining it.

It is not, first of all, against governments that it is important to rebel but against the human condition. Many young people, impassioned by the Revolution, exhaust in politics the revolt which at first should have transformed them.

For our "desiring will," as Blondel said, will always exceed our "determined will." As soon as we compare no matter what to our appetite, deep-seated in the infinite; as soon as we have measured the poverty of no matter what being, in comparison to our élan, we are freed of it, we have "classified" it. And all things, even the best, every being, even the most beloved, we will someday evaluate.

Thus it is that the most sensible and most intelligent people are the most often tempted to suicide: better than most people they measure the unbearable distance between what they are living and what they really are. Jacques Rivière wrote:

> In the evening, at the moment of retiring, the weary man looks at his day, and sees a lack in all his actions, a void between what he has done and what he had resolved to do... We have applied ourselves in vain: there is a slight, constant unhappiness with all our undertakings... There is always between ourselves and our soul, a subtle, discouraging difference.

Woe to those who are not aware of it!

Society and the churches have been cruelly blind towards these "unbalanced" persons.[2] No doubt, they are unbalanced, but is it not noble in them to be conscious of a state which is common to all of us? We, who claim to be stable and self-controlled, what have we thrown into the scale to balance our infinite vocation; money, fleshly indulgence, alcohol, power, unconsciousness?

The more sails a ship has, the faster it is capable of sailing ahead, of distance, of discoveries. But also, in proportion to the number of sails, it is vulnerable and threatened. We, who have taken in our sails, clipped our wings, limited our demands, how can we dare to despise them "who did not have the courage" to be content with an existence as mediocre as ours? There is much more cowardice in the attachment of certain men to their self-preservation than in the suicide of Samson, of Cato, or of Seneca.

*   *   *

Adolescence is the time when suicide is a temptation because it is the age when the aspirations are the widest and accomplishments the narrowest, the age when the human condition is resented most keenly and indignantly.

Indeed, intervening also at this period of confusion, are fear of the future (who would not be terrified by the threat of a future similar to that of many adults?), the refusal of risk, intolerance for suffering, the desire to avoid the trials of living and of settling into stability. But these reasons would be inoperative if the adolescent did not draw his strength from the perception of his interior richness, a wealth which is by no means a past which he would like to immobilize, but an aspiration which he already knows to be non realizable.

Suicide is not essentially despair; it is a refusal to surrender, a preference, an appeal, an attempt to find an escape beyond all hopes.

The appropriate way to avert suicide is not to accuse those who are disheartened with life of cowardice. It is to explain to them such an act will not change anything fundamentally, that they will find themselves, on the other side with the same necessity to construct a future despite unreasonableness, and that there would be nothing worse than to exchange their present abundant dissatisfaction with a future sterile satisfaction.

Man, in reality, does not die. He either constructs or destroys himself forever. Stormy youth so much fears being swallowed up by mediocrity that it renounces the opportunity to build itself—but it is self-deception to want to destroy exactly that which reveals itself as inextinguishable, insatiable.

There is only one duty: to live a true life, to continually reestablish a balance ceaselessly endangered, to renew its inspiration, to discover its being.

*   *   *

But it must be recognized that, when this duty becomes impossible or is accomplished, one has the right to choose his death.

Up to now, man has died like an animal, without wishing it, often without knowing it, "death in spite of himself," as could be written on so many tombs. And frequently, he dies disgraced, degraded. Too soon or too late.

"The fulfillment of personal existence coincides only rarely with death," write Landsberg in his essay on the experience of death. That is why all the resources of science must be employed to avoid premature deaths, but also, slow deaths. Man must be able to die humanely, that is, freely, at his own time, by his choice, at his peak. Christ is a free man, he died freely: "I give my life. I have the power to give it and the power to take it back. That is why the Father loves me: because I am giving my life."

Most certainly, let us not evade the people and tasks which need us. But there comes an hour when one has completed one's work, when one is a burden rather than a support and when it is just and charitable to cede to those who follow a vital space more and more coveted and restricted.

The deepest need of man is the need for Transcendence, the drive to give himself, to offer himself, to cast himself beyond self and even out of this twilight world, towards another world to explore and love.

Why not quit the trampoline of our earthly existence while it still permits us to bounce, instead of waiting until one can no longer topple from it?

Let us examine how primitive we still are by imagining a person who appreciates life, who has lived it fully, but who deliberately orients himself towards another mode of life of which this life has given him a foretaste and a desire. A death like that, a free death, would it not be completely human? When will it be written in the Declaration of Human Rights that each person must prepare means of developing his life, and also of terminating it at a certain age if he judges it advantageous?

Euthanasia

We have said (chapter 1) that life, and even human life is not a supreme value to preserve in preference to all others. We thus shock many of our contemporaries. For want of something positive, they would like to place at least this limit to the unatonable struggles which are engaged in among them, the absolutes of displacement, Marxism, fascism, anarchism, racism, and...liberalism. Our societies have lost their religious or patriotic cement — the war of 1940 was already a strife of ideologies rather than nationalisms — and our citizens have become as much strangers one to another as animals of different species. Because, with man, it is not instinct, but the recognition of a spiritual solidarity which ties people together.

But this meritorious relationship is impeded by insoluble dilemmas. Each political decision (and not only war), each social or economic one is an authorization of life for certain people, and a sentence of death for others. The regulations concerning highway speed condemn or save thousands of drivers. The laws regarding tobacco, alcohol, are choices between life and death. Economic reasons oblige us to select the beneficiaries of transplants, kidneys, lungs or artificial hearts, or of prolonged comas. More simply yet, the modicum of pensions granted to the old accelerates, without doubt until the assistance disappears. And the sanctioning of abortion prefigures a law for euthanasia. Are not the embryos of life worth more than the waste products?

Our civilization imposes choices: Who should live, who should die? Every doctor can, from now on, be accused of nonassistance to a person in danger if he has not used the new techniques for delaying death. But we prefer to leave to the doctors the responsibilities which go beyond them and a power which terrifies them.

Humane people generally agree not to interfere if there is no reasonable hope of recovery and to be satisfied with the basic care which permits the invalid to die in a decent manner. But we hesitate to take from the patient the means of survival because we feel we are killing that person.

However, the difference is very small. Is it more serious not to connect an electrical apparatus or to disconnect it?

People authorize the doctor to soften the end for the invalid by analgesics which hasten death, which are not given to quicken the end but to prevent a long deterioration, or just to economize on the exorbitant cost of continuing the treatments. People allow drugs which alleviate pain even though they are physically and mentally harmful, but not those which would cut short this degeneration.

We are for actual euthanasia upon the reflected and insisted request of the patient, in case of unbearable pain or of progressive deterioration.

Man has a right over his life. Possible abuse of that right is not a reason for suppressing it. Old people, incurables, ought to be provided with an efficacious and painless means of ending life, by themselves when they deem it proper, or with the aid of others when they are no longer capable of it. In case of unconsciousness a previous statement should be respected and carried out when there no longer remains a reasonable hope of return to health. If such a statement be lacking, one should have recourse to the doctors, the medical team and to a lawyer.

Respect for life is exceeded by respect for the person who wishes to die with dignity. It is not the length of life which counts but its quality. In many cases the doctor should no longer preserve life at any cost, but be a good midwife assisting death. His vocation "to the service of life" and his medical duties are limited by the rights of the invalid to dispose of his person and to be served as long as he chooses it.

NOTES

[1] The legend of the scorpion which kills itself has been destroyed by Lucien Berland in his book *Les Scorpions* (Stock 1945).

[2] They excommunicated them or refused them a Christian burial. In England, even today, if they misfire at themselves, they are liable to imprisonment and everywhere they are saved and revived without regard for their wishes.

The "theological" reason for this attitude is the old despotic conception of the divinity. God is the master of life and of death. Man does not have rights over his life nor his body. They have only been lent to him by an economical God who will take them back at his wish, as absolute proprietor. It is for this reason that for a long time the transplant of organs was condemned: to give a kidney to his brother was to usurp the divine privileges and to commit a mortal sin.

As if freedom, which is the proper quality of humans, did not extend to himself, and as if charity did not surpass all law, did not justify in certain cases mutilation or suicide. (The Church recognizes it however, in one case: for the benefit of virginity only, the defense of which would authorize suicide.)

As for the state, in the ancient city as in modern collectivistic society, it asserted, likewise, its right as proprietor over the citizen who is only an instrument in the service of the community.

God no more determined the end of our lives than he established the beginning. God has made man free. Let us assume our responsibilities!

CHAPTER 7

Crossing the Border

Death is the last test of our faith in life.

To live is to believe, that is to say, to give trust; it is to consent to wait for what one does not yet see and to give it time to disclose itself.

In the most important decisions of life (choice of a profession, of a spouse, of fellowship, of having a child), reason aids us, but is never sufficient. Our most careful calculations ought to be completed, uplifted by confidence, which is the best guarantee of success.

A man can not live by what he sees or knows. He can only exist on what he hopes. A child is fascinating because of the promise which it represents. In pressing it against us, we are embracing more what it will become than what it now is. A child which could not grow, a baby for whom no development can be expected, would destroy all interest, would be a catastrophe. Basically, a child is worth only the hopes that one places in it. Its established worth is nothing in comparison with what it will become. If you bring a child into the world, you are making an immense act of faith, you are opening yourself up to expectation.

Marriage is an identical wager. Who can guarantee the success of it, who can assure its duration, if this be not love, which is defined as, "to trust in the other forever"? The spouses love one another so much as to create each other; so much do they trust, so much do they expect miracles of each other which no other person could bring them.

At death, as at marriage, we are challenged: "Do you trust or do you refuse it? Do you open yourself or do you prefer to close up? Do you withdraw into your wealth, your possessions, into your past or do you launch out toward the future?"

Have not all your preceding experiences convinced you that life has more resources than you could suspect of it? Have you had to repent of the trust which you have placed in life? Have you not had countless confirmations that you did well to believe in your love, to hope in your children, to persevere in spite of difficulties, to believe beyond all appearances?

In this last test, why would you repudiate yourself? Death is an invention of life. You would not feel this anguish in face of death, if you would not, by your rejection, interfere with the very movement of life in you. You maladjust yourself. You stifle the spring, the breathing of your faith. Will death be the first happening of your existence that you approach with no hope?

Real death, is not dying, it is to stop believing, to stop growing, to stop being born . . . and people stop at all ages.

True life, is to continue to hope even in confronting death.